Directory-Enabled Networks

Directory-Enabled Networks

Marcus Goncalves

McGraw-Hill

New York   San Francisco   Washington, D.C.
Auckland   Bogotá   Caracas   Lisbon   London
Madrid   Mexico City   Milan   Montreal   New Delhi
San Juan   Singapore   Sydney   Tokyo   Toronto

McGraw-Hill

A Division of The McGraw·Hill Companies

1 2 3 4 5 6 7 8 9 0   AGM/AGM   9 0 4 3 2 1 0 9

ISBN 0-07-134951-0

The sponsoring editor for this book was Simon Yates and the production supervisor
was Clare Stanley. It was set in Esprit by Patricia Wallenburg.

Printed and bound by Quebecor/Martinsburg.

McGraw-Hill books are available at special quantity discounts to use as premiums and
sales promotions, or for use in corporate training programs. For more information,
please write to the Director of Special Sales, McGraw-Hill, 11 West 19th Street,
New York, NY 10011. Or contact your local bookstore.

 This book is printed on recycled, acid-free paper containing
a minimum of 50% recycled, de-inked fiber.

Dedication

To my forever-beautiful wife Carla for all her support and sacrifice during the production of this book, and my awesome kids Samir, Andrea and Joshua, for giving me so much joy as a parent. To God be the glory.

Marcus Goncalves

Acknowledgments

I must acknowledge a great debt of gratitude to the authors and professionals working on DEN, in particular the Desktop Management Task Force, for discussing DEN's development and being a valuable source of information on DEN. A complete list of authors and their individual contributions is too extensive for this forum, but the Bibliography at the end of this book contains a list of resources and their authors.

I gratefully acknowledge Xinzhong Yu for sharing with me his work in progress. I thank John Strassner, of Cisco for authorizing me to use DEN specification (v3.0c5). I also thank Steven Judd and Bernard Abobe, of Microsoft, for sharing with me their expertise on the subject and allowing me to use some of their work.

I thank 3Com and Cisco for authorizing me to use a couple of their whitepapers. Particular thanks to Frank Fuller for granting me permission to use some of 3Com's materials and helping me to get additional information. I thank Mike Cookish and Martin Barclay for their priceless help. I also gratefully acknowledge the assistance of Monish Rajpal, of John Hopkins University, for allowing me to use his work on QoS.

I would like to thank Simon Yates of McGraw-Hill for his confidence in me during this project.

Glory be to God, for allowing me to contribute to a better multimedia virtual world in this way.

Contents

PART I

THE TECHNOLOGY

PART II

THE IMPLEMENTATION PROCESS

        The Role of Policy-Powered Networks1   103
            Benefits of Policy-Powered Networking   *105*
        Delivering Policy-Powered Networks   105
            The Four Types of Policy-Enforcement Devices   *107*
        Policy Transaction Models   110
            Active Policy Device: Layer 3 Packet Filtering   *110*
            Active Policy Device: Desktop CoS   *112*
            Passive Policy Device: Modify Default Queue Mapping *113*

7   UNDERSTANDING QUALITY OF SERVICE   117

        What Is QoS?   119
            A Word About Flow   *122*
        Role of Quality of Service   125
            Quality of Service Characteristics   *127*
            Managing Quality of Service   *127*
            Quality of Service Challenges   *131*
            Potential Issues in Implementing a QoS System in DEN *134*
        Class of Service   135

8   DIRECTORY-BASED QOS MANAGEMENT   137

        QoS Models   138
        Management Services   139
            Remote Appliance Management   *139*
        Admission Control Services   142
            Understanding Windows QoS   *145*
            Development of APIs   *147*

Preface

The directory-enabled network (DEN) specification forms the basis of an implementer's agreement in support of immediate customer requirements for leveraging network services and ensuring interoperability between networking applications of different vendors. Since Microsoft and Cisco teamed up for the development of DEN, much has been announced and discussed, but DEN's specifications are still being developed.

This book discusses the rapid specification of DEN as a directory services information model and schema, and how it can facilitate the interoperability of distributed applications, management tools, and network elements. It also discusses the challenges to both Microsoft and Cisco's teams to deliver the specs, especially after Cisco and Microsoft forwarded it to the Desktop Management Task Force (DMTF). Since then DEN has rapidly progressed, with significant input from the Ad Hoc Working Group comprised of over 300 industry and customer advocates. It has been incorporated into the CIM workgroup.

This book also discusses more complex DEN challenges including a detailed information model for name forms, structure rules, matching rules, and syntax, as well as naming policies and how to constrain the Directory Information Tree (DIT), Management of profiles and policies by group, and dealing with the issue of group-based policy.

The book is organized in three parts:

PART I—*The Technology*, is comprised of four chapters covering DEN's core technology.

Chapter 1, *Development of Directory-Enabled Networks*, rationalizes DEN and explains why DEN is necessary. It also provides an overview of the vendors involved in development of DEN as the role of the DMTF.

Chapter 2, *Defining DEN*, provides a comprehensive overview of DEN's base schema, its class hierarchy and extension, and the information model.

Chapter 3, *The Common Information Model*, defines CIM and its role on DEN, as well as the management challenges it faces. The chapter discusses how CIM works and its specification.

Chapter 4, *An Overview of Important Specifications*, focuses on the Light Directory Access Protocol (LDAP) and the security aspects of DEN. It discusses the dynamic attributes and schema for RADIUS as well as the Routing Policy Specification Language (RPSL) and the Integration of IPSec on DEN

PART II, *The Implementation Process*, is comprised of another four chapters discussing DEN's implementation issues.

Chapter 5, *Policy Powered Networks*, discusses the role of Policy Powered Networks (PPN), the policy transaction model and planning for it. It also discusses the Application Specific Classification Policy (ASPC).

Chapter 6, *Directory Services*, discusses how to use the directory services and their support of quality of service (QoS), as well as payment handler, delivery and other services.

Chapter 7, *Understanding Quality of Service*, extends the discussion of QoS, its role, challenges and progress.

Chapter 8, *Directory Based QoS Management*, looks at the management aspects of QoS, from models and policy components to admission control services and policy framework.

Chapter 9, *Protecting Mission-Critical Application*, discusses the implementation of mission-critical applications over the network and the questions of IP precedence, weighted fair queuing, frame relay priority PVC, enabling desktop video, among other topics.

PART III, *DEN at Work: Challenges and the Latest Developments*, consists of one chapter and appendix which provides resources and updates about DEN as of the publication date of this book.

Chapter 10, *Remote Access Schema*, provides an overview of remote access in DEN, covering profile and policy objects, extensibility, authentication and dynamic attributes.

Appendix A is a comprehensive glossary of terms

Audience

The professionals most likely to take advantage of this book are:

+ Computer-literate professionals who graduated at least a few years age and are concerned about the turns and advances electronic commerce is taking

- ✦ Programmers/analysts/software developers, engineers/test engineers and project managers
- ✦ MIS and IS&T (Information systems and Technology) professionals
- ✦ Professionals involved with setting up, implementing and managing extranets and virtual stores
- ✦ Webmasters
- ✦ Entry-level (in terms of computer literacy) professionals who want to understand how the Internet works and how Internet commerce develops
- ✦ Advanced computer-literate people who might use this book as a quick reference tool.

PART I

The Technology

CHAPTER 1

Directory Services

Directory services are fundamental in creating intelligent networks. Physically distributed, a directory service is logically centralized to work as a repository of infrequently changing data used to manage a computing environment. Directory services can be very helpful in managing increasingly complex networks. As the number of different types of network elements increases, and each runs a different set of protocols and services over different media, interoperability and management become almost impossible. The directory offers the promise of being a central repository for storing and retrieving all information.

Using Directory Services

A traditional directory service provides a means for locating and identifying users and available resources in a distributed system. Directory services also provide the foundation for adding, modifying, removing, renaming, and managing system components without disrupting the services provided by other system components. Directory services can be used to:

+ Store information about system components in a distributed manner. The directory is replicated among several servers so that a user or service needing access to information stored in the directory can query a local server for the information.
+ Support white pages and yellow pages lookup
+ Allow single user logon to network services, thereby using system and network resources and applications
+ Enable a location-independent point of administration and management
+ Replicate data to provide consistent access. Modifications made to any replica of the directory are propagated around the network so that any application accessing the directory anywhere sees consistent information after the change is propagated.

As PCs become more powerful, people are finding more ways to take advantage of the power of their computers. Residential customers

---

This chapter was based on 3Com's Directory Enabled Networks – Information Model and Base Schema. For more information check 3Com's site at URL **http://www.3com.com**.

want rich multimedia services, such as data and video. Corporate customers are looking to telcos and service providers for powerful yet affordable services. Users want a reliable, easy-to-use, friendly service.

There is a fundamental shift toward bandwidth-intensive and isochronous network applications. Current directory services technology is not designed to meet the ever-increasing demands of today's public and private network applications because they were built mainly to accommodate administrative needs.

The key to satisfying these growing customer needs is to switch to a new paradigm for using directory services. The directory must be transformed from a "dumb warehouse" to an authoritative, distributed, intelligent repository of information for services and applications.

The directory is the foundation for an intelligent infrastructure. Bandwidth-intensive and isochronous network applications require that the devices lying on a path through the network between source and sink be configured appropriately in order to function properly. This configuration is often dynamic, taking place on demand when a particular user logs onto the network from any of a number of possible locations. Only when management information about the users, network devices, and services involved is available in a single, authoritative location can this diverse information be inter-related. This inter-relation is critical to effective managment of this emerging class of applications.

Purpose and Scope

A discussion of purpose and scope should define the problem domains, information model, usage, and detailed directory schema for integrating networks with directory services. It is an initiative driven by equipment vendors, independent software vendors and customers to define a rational, usable model for enhancing the usability and manageability of networks via integration with the directory service. In these networks, the network resources (devices, operating systems, management tools, and applications) use the directory service to:

+ Publish information about themselves
+ Discover other resources
+ Obtain information about other resources.

The directory service becomes the hub around which the distributed system turns; the degree of cooperation among network components and distributed applications is dramatically enhanced. The result is a network in which service to users is predictable and repeatable, security is strengthened, and management is easier.

Administrative needs and the tools that service them have evolved as distributed systems have evolved. Today's directory services were designed to provide central management of security and contact information in a network with a relatively small number of relatively large computers. Network management has been the province of more specialized tools, each with its own information store. Application management has been addressed as an afterthought, when it was addressed at all.

Convergence of the information stores holding the universe of management information has been difficult. The current environment is one where vertical management tools have proliferated. Lack of integration and the sheer complexity of the tools themselves has become a barrier to the deployment of new applications as well as the exchange and sharing of data captured by these individual network management and provisioning tools.

Administrators need a level of control over their networks that is currently unavailable. Streaming multimedia, use of public networks and attendant security concerns, and rapidly growing user communities present a tremendous challenge.

Simply managing individual devices is no longer sufficient. Network administrators need to define and manage policies to control the network and its resources in a distributed, yet logically centralized, manner. In general terms, policies define what resources a given consumer can use in the context of a given application or service. Inability to manage policies easily is a significant barrier to deployment of current and emerging distributed applications.

Defining and managing policies requires a common store of well-defined information about the network and its resources: users, applications, devices, protocols, media, services and the relationships among these elements. This is information about the network as well as the information traditionally viewed as defining the network. At issue is where to store policy and other information that needs to be applied across components in a way that makes it usable by a broad range of consumers.

A scalable, secure directory service that presents a logically centralized view of physically distributed information is the logical place to store the "meta-information" essential to creating and managing a next-generation network. The specification for the integration of directory services and network services defines the information model and schema to make this possible.

The Need for a Directory-Enabled Network

Directory-enabled networks (DEN) must:

1. Bind users to services available from the network according to a consistent and rational set of policies
2. Provide the foundation to build intelligent networks and network-enabled applications

Both these needs require network-enabled applications that can access diverse information from a common logical repository. That repository uses the directory as a centralized information store that coordinates information storage and retrieval, enabling other data- and application-specific repositories to be united. Eventually, intelligent network applications will transparently leverage the appropriate information about the network and the services it offers on behalf of the user. The development of intelligent networks can be achieved through the following steps:

1. Development of a robust directory service that is DEN-compliant for storing network element and service information
2. Definition of an extensible information model that represents the structural, behavioral and functional relationships between objects in the schema
3. Adding protocols for accessing, managing and manipulating directory information.

The goals of the directory-enabled network development work are to:

✦ Address customer requirements to provide transparent support for applications that have the ability to leverage the network infrastructure on behalf of the end-user

✦ Provide a robust, extensible foundation for building network-enabled applications that model:
  ✧ Network elements and services
  ✧ Physical and logical network topology
  ✧ How the network functions
✦ Provide significant benefit for a selected set of network-enabled applications, including:
  ✧ Inventory management
  ✧ Asset management
  ✧ Configuration and provisioning applications
  ✧ Capacity planning
✦ Provide a foundation for the creation, provisioning and management of end-to-end network services on a per-user basis
✦ Provide a basis for the definition, application, and management of policies that control network-wide services.

According to 3Com, customer attendees at the initial Directory-enabled Networks workshop (held November 4, 1997) submitted a list of requirements, as shown in Figure 1.1.

CIM Influence

The Common Information Model (CIM) is discussed in more detail in Chapter 4, but here is a list of critical concepts CIM provides for DEN:

✦ **Product, FRU, etc:** CIM defines a collection of classes (Product, FRU, etc.) that represent a product and replaceable parts of a product. DEN will not use these per se, but applications based on DEN, such as inventory, asset tracking and capacity planning, will use them. They are therefore included for completeness.
✦ **ManagedSystemElement:** CIM uses this as the base class for any system or system component that should be managed. It is the superclass of PhysicalElement and LogicalElement, which are the base classes for defining physical and logical characteristics of system components. This is a critical part of DEN, as all the DEN classes corresponding to managing the physical and logical aspects of network elements are derived from CIM's PhysicalElement and LogicalElement classes, respectively.

Intranet – provisioning, managing, securing.
Internet service management (includes service creation and network element provisioning).
Service Management – DNS, DKCP, DS, RADIUS, QoS, Authentication and Authorization, PKI, incorporating policy decisions to control access to and allocation of resources and services available on the network.
Service Management in a VPN environment: QoS WAN over Internet, etc.
End to End security of applications over the network.
Enable the merging of user and group (e.g., people) administration with physical network configuration and administration.
Support for mobile/roaming users requires pages of access control lists and volumes of manually administered router and switch configurations — this needs to be addressed by DEN.
Infrastructure for developers to write intelligent "network aware" applications that can leverage network capabilities and services.
User-specific profiles that "follow" the user instead of profiles that are tied to a physical port or an IP address. Ties back to support for roaming users.
Network authentication and authorization for applications and services.
Manage network policies across the entire enterprise.
Provide infrastructure to configure and manage VPNs for individuals and workgroups.
Provide infrastructure for authentication and authorization for devices and users; move beyond RADIUS to incorporate PK. PKI for users and workgroups; management of ACLs and filters, other services.
Configuring devices based on policy and profile.
Managing higher layer protocols and applications.
PKI management: CAs, certificates, enrollment.
Encryption/Cypher management.
Inventory and asset tracking.

FIGURE 1.1   List of requirements submitted by customers during DEN workshop in November 1997

◆ **Configuration:** CIM defines a Configuration and a Setting class. The Configuration class defines a group of settings that collectively represent a certain behavior or desired functional state of a ManagedSystemElement. DEN will extend this concept to model the configuration and provisioning of network elements and services.

✦ **Service:** CIM defines two important concepts, Service and ServiceAccessPoint, that are critical to defining network services. A Service is defined as a logical element that contains the information necessary to represent and manage functionality provided by a device and/or software feature. A service is a general-purpose object to configure and manage the implementation of functionality. It is not the functionality itself.

   A ServiceAccessPoint is defined as the management aspects of the ability to utilize or invoke a Service. Both these concepts are derived from the LogicalElement class, which is a subclass from ManagedSystemElement. DEN will refine this basic description to focus on the definition, management and delivery of *network services* while keeping compatibility with the Service and ServiceAccessPoint classes.

✦ **Software:** CIM defines the general notion of software using the SoftwareFeature and SoftwareElement classes. Both are derived from the LogicalElement class. SoftwareFeature is used to describe a function or capability of a product or an application. SoftwareElement represents the individually manageable portions of the SoftwareFeature class. DEN will refine this concept, in conjunction with System, Check and Action (see below) to address the specific requirements of network elements and services.

✦ **System:** CIM defines a rich system hierarchy. The System class is derived from LogicalElement, and is an enumerable aggregation of a set of objects that operate as a functional whole. ComputerSystem is derived from System and represents a specialized collection of components that have computing capabilities and serve as an aggregation point for components such as file systems and operating systems. DEN will use the concepts of System, ComputerSystem, OperatingSystem, FileSystem, and other classes to realize the concept of a logical network element.

✦ **Location:** CIM defines a Location class that specifies the address and location of a physical element. DEN expands on this concept to address concepts like: the "engineering router" is in this wiring closet on this floor of this building.

✦ **Check and Action:** CIM defines two top-level classes, Check and Action, that are used for SoftwareElements. A Check is a condition or characteristic that is expected to be true for a given computer system. An Action is an operation that completely or partly transitions a given software element to its next state or removes that software element from its current state. DEN will use these concepts, along with already defined subclasses of Check and Action, to augment notions of configuration and reboot of network devices. More advanced concepts (e.g., the checks of a Policy) await the definition of Rules by the DMTF.

✦ **Application:** CIM also defines the notion of an application. It adds the concept that an application (or software system) is used to support a particular business function. As such, it can be managed as an independent unit. The aspect of managing the application means that it can be separated into a set of components, each of which can be managed. DEN incorporates these concepts and adds them to the notion of application as defined by the X.500 directory structure.

CHAPTER **2**

The Development of Directory-Enabled Networks

DEN is still a new concept, describing mechanisms that should enable network devices such as routers and switches to access and use directory information to implement another new concept, now known as a *policy-powered network* (PPN). PPNs are discussed in Chapter 5. For now, just keep in mind that PPNs' main scope is to associate information about individual users, groups, organizational units, entire organizations and even events (such as the closing of the fiscal year of a company) with various network services or classes of service.

Therefore, the purpose of DEN and PPN is to attend to both users' and applications' specific needs as well to enhance network management. The core technologies necessary to achieve this goal are directory and directory services.

However, in the tradition of the IT market, market reality has lagged behind the hype of the media and the excitement of those supporting the standard. Lucent, for example, convinced of the many benefits proposed by DEN, is beginning to deploy its own version of the standard, the Internet Directory Server (IDS). Lucent is a member of the DMTF's DEN initiative and fully supports it, but as with IPv6 and some of Java's implementations, vendors have begun implementing partial features of these new technologies before the marketplace could catch up.

The risk is a lack of standard or the existence of several versions of the same basic implementation. In DEN's case, this could be fatal for the standard. Fortunately, the DMTF is in control and pushing the standard in a timely fashion, and at the same time, making sure there is broad vendor support for it.

Introduction

Directory Enabled Networks, are networks where users and applications interact in a controlled way; network elements and network services provide predictable and repeatable services to users, while also strengthening security and simplifying provisioning and management of network resources. Initiated by Cisco and Microsoft, DEN is supported in the industry by many companies. The information model and base schema of DEN are derived from CIM and X.500, with added new concepts. The model structure is object oriented. DEN uses LDAP to access, manage, and manipulate directory information.

As the Internet penetrates the enterprise networks and intranets become extranets, networks as a whole are becoming increasingly complex. There are different types of network elements, each running a potentially different set of protocols and services over possibly different media. Consequently, a network has too many different directory services for network administrators to manage successfully. For example, there are operating system directories, RADIUS directories, DNS directories, DHCP directories, etc. Administering all of these directories might be a big headache and time consuming, because of different user interfaces, incompatible data formats, and many other problems.

It was in September 1997 that Cisco Systems Inc. and Microsoft Corp. launched the DEN initiative. Since then, DEN has rapidly progressed. At the time of their writing, DEN has gone through two reviews, with significant input from the Ad Hoc Working Group of over 300 industry and customer advocates.

During Spring 1998 Microsoft and Cisco were already announcing the establishment of the DEN initiative as an industry standard. At the time, the perceived importance of DEN was such that the Directory-Enabled Networks Ad Hoc Working Group (DEN AHWG) had decided, through the DEN Customer Advisory Group, to submit DEN specification to the DMTF standards body.

As a standard body, the DMTF includes entities such as Charles Schwab & Company Inc., Sprint Corp., Texaco Inc. and the University of Washington, all helping to guide the content of the DEN specification and the timing of its submission as a standard. In September 1998 the DMTF announced its acceptance of the DEN specification from DEN AHWG Customer Advisory Board and its incorporation to DMTF's Common Information Model (CIM) standard for enterprise management. CIM aims to define the rules and categories for an information model that provides a common way to describe and share management information enterprisewide.

Since the work already done with DEN fits well within DMTF's CIM specification, DEN has been incorporated into CIM. Ray Williams of Tivoli Systems Inc. chairs CIM's Technology Development Committee.

From the start, DEN has been an open, customer-driven initiative. Since DEN's review process moved to the DMTF, vendors and customers now have an open forum and process to facilitate standardization of the DEN specification. This will help vendors and customers to benefit from a unified model for integrating users, applications and network services.

Companies already involved with DEN:

+ 3COM Corp.
+ ActiveLane
+ Arrowpoint Communications Inc.
+ Bay Networks
+ Berkeley Networks
+ Cabletron Systems
+ Cisco Systems
+ Compuserve Network Services
+ Cylink Corp.
+ Hewlett-Packard Co.
+ OpenView Division
+ IBM
+ ISOCOR
+ Lucent Technologies
+ MetaInfo Inc.
+ Microsoft
+ Netscape Communications
+ Orchestream
+ Process Software Corp.
+ Quadritek Systems Inc.
+ RedCreek Communications Inc.
+ Siemens-Nixdorf Informationssysteme AG
+ SwitchSoft Systems Inc.
+ TIBCO Software
+ TimeStep Corp.
+ Ukiah Software Inc.

This chapter discusses DEN and how it can benefit networks and information exchange.

Understanding What a Directory Service Is

Directory services provide the foundation for creating intelligent networks. As a physically distributed, logically centralized repository of networks and general computing management information, directory services can store all those infrequently changing data and make them available to network administrators and systems professionals.

As networks grow in complexity, an increasing number of different types of network elements and heterogeneous platforms, as well as a diversity of protocols, media and scope, have taken a major toll on management and the ability to internetwork. Network professionals need a common interface, a standard tool that enables them to store and retrieve network inherent information when necessary, regardless of their location. A directory service offers this capability.

Typically, a directory service enables a user to locate and identify other users and other networkable resources in a distributed system. Directory services also provide the foundation for adding, modifying, removing, renaming, and managing system components without disrupting the services provided by other system components. These directories can:

✦ Serve as a distributed repository of information about system components. Through directory replication between servers a user can query and retrieve information about a network resource from anywhere on that network.

✦ Support cataloging systems, such as inventory of printers, document management, etc.

✦ Allow single-user logon to network services, thereby using system and network resources and applications

✦ Enable a location-independent point of administration and management without having to centralize administrative tools

✦ Replicate data to provide consistent access. Modifications made to any replica of the directory are propagated around the network so that any application accessing the directory anywhere sees consistent information after the change is propagated.

As computer users rely more and more on the power of the computer and as the network becomes the PC, the Internet becomes the common "mega-network" interconnecting the smaller networks, the

PCs. This new Internet-based client/server model requires a more robust, scalable and secure directory services. Home computing demands a variety of processes and networking-intense services, from multimedia services, such as data and video, to researching and messaging services. Business computing requires powerful services, coupled with reliability, user-friendliness and low cost. Unfortunately, current directory services technology was not designed for such bandwidth-intensive and distributed applications.

There is an emerging need for a directory service than can be authoritative, distributed, and capable of becoming an intelligent repository of information for services and applications. Administrators need a level of control over their networks that is currently unavailable. Streaming multimedia, use of public networks and attendant security concerns, and rapidly growing user communities present a tremendous challenge.

Bandwidth-intensive network applications require a dynamic configuration of devices, according to each particular user's needs. In order to provide a user with the resources required after logging onto a network, management information about the user, network devices, and services involved must be available in a single, authoritative location so this information can be related and managed.

Why Directory-Enabled Network?

In today's Internet-based network computing, a directory service becomes the hub around which the distributed system revolves, dramatically enhancing the degree of cooperation among network components and distributed applications. The result is a network in which service to users is predictable and repeatable, security is strengthened, and management is easier.

As network managers begin to rely more and more on policies to control the network and its resources, these policies need to be redefined. Basically, policies define what resources (applications or services) a user has available. These policies must be manageable, as otherwise the development of distributed applications may suffer. Also, defining and managing policies requires a common store of well-defined information about the network and its resources: users, applications, devices, protocols, media, services and the relationships among these elements.

A scalable, secure directory service that presents a logically centralized view of physically distributed information is the logical place to store the "meta-information" essential to creating and managing a next-generation network. The specification for the integration of directory services and network services defines the information model and schema to make this possible.

However, characterizing and controlling network elements and services is inherently complex. As discussed earlier in this chapter, information needs to be organized to allow different users and applications to use it. Existing tools and applications focus on managing individual network elements rather than on a collection of network elements that is itself an entity. This specification defines a standard schema for storing persistent state; and an information model, discussed in Chapter 3, for describing the relationships among objects representing users, applications, network elements and network services.

The DEN Initiative

The DEN initiative is intended to integrate the management of servers and network services as well as to enable a new generation of networked applications. The DEN specification forms the basis of an implementers' agreement in support of immediate customer requirements for leveraging network services and ensuring interoperability between networking applications of different vendors.

DEN enables user profiles, applications and network services to integrate through a common information model that stores network state and exposes network information. This information enables optimization of bandwidth use. It also allows for policy-based management and provides a single point of administration for all the network resources. DEN helps corporations lower total cost of ownership (TCO) and improves the level of network services available for users, regardless of their physical location.

CIM lays the framework for managing entire enterprise computing environments in a way that enables the sharing and integration of information between diverse data sources and management systems. DEN integrates knowledge about user profiles, applications and network services to allow for a new class of intelligent networked applications and provide users with a full range of services, regardless of their location. Thus, DEN builds upon CIM to model the functionality and management of network elements and services. The resulting common schema will enable the increasing integration of management services.

DEN's draft specification, as suggested by its name, provides a schema and information model for representing the network elements and services in a directory. The specification aims to establish an association between the network services, users and applications. A set of data models for typical network devices is defined by the specification, which also implements these extensions to the directory services schema. This means management tools can populate the directory with instances of actual devices found on the network. Properties to be set, including descriptions of the services supported by the devices discovered on the network, as well as provisioning and/or configuration details.

DEN enables networks to be dynamically configured according to individual user needs. For instance, certain users may be authorized to use the network for video conferencing, which will require secure links between points, while others can only print or check their e-mail. This is only possible through the establishment of a common data store for the tools used to authenticate and authorize applications and services for the user and network extensions. This network-enabled directory provides a unified focal point for the administration, management, and use of tools and applications.

John Strassner, co-author of the DEN specification, has emphasized the importance of moving standardization of DEN onto DMTF from the beginning of the initiative, while DEN was still under DEN AHWG auspices. He understood how crucial this was for the wide adoption of the DEN. Merging DEN onto CIM's efforts ensured that DEN would be an extension model of CIM. In addition, DEN's specification provided an excellent basis for future work being done in the DMTF's CIM model. As noted by Ray Williams, the integration of DEN into the CIM Schema and the Web-Based Enterprise Management (WBEM) environment is going to benefit both customers and the industry, since it will be a cornerstone for service management. Therefore, many of the physical and device aspects of the DEN specification are being included in the CIM schema.

Characterizing and Controlling Network Elements

Characterizing and controlling network elements and services is inherently complex. Information needs to be organized to enable different people and applications to use it. DEN is being used as a starting point to ensure seamless integration with directory services.

The DMTF's networks working group is in the process of defining detailed schemata and a comprehensive information model that:

✦ Models LANs, MANs, WANs, system area networks, and storage networks elements and network services

✦ Identifies the network-centered elements and services involved in LANs, MANs, WANs, system area networks, and storage networks for definition by the Systems and Devices working group

✦ Identifies the network-centered services involved in LANs, MANs, WANs, system area networks, and storage networks for definition by the User Definition working group and creates the specific extensions to the service framework as required to support naming, resolution, and discovery

✦ Defines the associations that enable clients, such as users, applications, and host machines, to be bound to services that are available on the network based on the definition of a policy framework that associates the needs of users with network mechanisms

✦ Describes the relationships between different types of network elements and services

✦ Addresses structural, behavioral, and functional models of network elements and services

✦ Models network states, such as current, desired, alternative, failed, etc.

✦ Models logical and physical network topology including the flow of data and its control

✦ Works with the User Definition working group on profiles that define the association between user and network policies

✦ Identifies security-related requirements as input to the Technical Development Committee.

The Networks working group is in the process of defining the following four fundamental knowledge domains:

✦ **Physical connectivity:** A model of the physical connections between components
✦ **Logical connectivity:** An idealized view of the network
✦ **Physical containment:** A model of the location and spatial relationships of components
✦ **Logical containment:** The intersection of network elements and services with business organizations.

These knowledge domains enable the application to learn and navigate a physical or logical network topology, such as virtual subnet configuration, by using objects that are independent from the underlying network media, access protocols, and physical hardware.

The Networks working group is also focusing on defining the relationships and associations between devices and network services and other CIM objects to facilitate, enhance, and define how different objects interact with each other.

Microsoft and Cisco Alliance

Cisco and Microsoft have done a good job of simplifying the complexity of dealing with network services and users. The alliance enabled the leverage of their own applications and integrated solutions.

However, DEN is not restricted to the windows platform. It is open and can be extended to provide access to other name spaces. Its cross-platform nature provides a common way to access heterogeneous platforms where directories reside. Active Directory (AD), which supports the native Windows 2000 (former Windows NT 5.0) name space, also supports access to DNS (Domain Name Service), NDS (Novell Directory Service), and X.500-based directories, using their native protocols, or LDAP.

Both DEN and Active Directory rely on LDAP as a core data access protocol. The same is true for LDAP, which is also fully supported in the Active Directory Services Interface (ADSI), enabling cross-platform compatibility between LDAP and Active Directory-based directories, as well as others.

TIP

ADSI is a set of open interfaces that abstracts the capabilities of directory services from different network providers to present a single view for accessing and managing network resources. Both administrators and developers can use ADSI services to enumerate and manage resources in a directory service, no matter which network environment contains the resource.

The major benefit from Microsoft and Cisco's alliance is that the extension of Active Directory in Windows 2000 to the network name space. Cisco will produce UNIX versions of the Active Directory. Microsoft and Cisco are ensuring full cross-platform directory services integrated with network services.

3Com's Work on DEN

3Com acknowledges the power of DEN and policy-powered networking in helping to simplify and automate many complex tasks related to the management of a large enterprise network, which may have too many different directory services for network administrators to manage. Supervising all these directories demands a lot of time and resources, since there tend to be different formats, duplication and inconsistency of user names, synchronization problems during data modification, etc. Certain information, such as user names, may also need to be entered many times, often in inconsistent formats.

DEN's ultimate goal is to establish a single directory structure accessible to the entire enterprise. The administration of this "mega-directory" could then be distributed into various management domains. IT departments would decide who has administrative right to update which part of the directory and so forth. Some administration could be done centrally, while others tasks could be distributed locally to enhance performance.

3Com's view of DEN revolves around its new way to support network management via scalable device configuration management and policy powered networking.

Scalable Device Configuration Management

Directory support for device configuration management allows network devices to retrieve their configuration parameters directly from a directory server. The benefits are obvious as the size and scope of an organization's network expands. If a network has many routers configured, when an additional one is introduced to the network, it will not have to be individually configured. Instead, the router will examine the directory for its configuration parameters and then go online on its on.

Centralized device configuration management will require that network managers store configuration parameters for each network node in a common directory service, as shown in Figure 2.1. In this scenario, the network manager places the appropriate attributes, such as IP address, subnet mask, default gateway and so forth, directly into the node's record in the directory service.

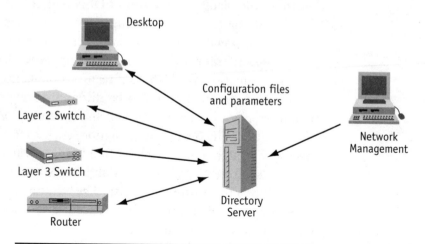

FIGURE 2.1   Centralized device configuration management

As shown in Figure 2.1, a unified directory service can dramatically enhance the level of service of networking simplify network management. DEN enables a sort of plug-and-play environment for networking.

Policy-Powered Networking

Policy-powered networking (PPN) is much more complex than device configuration management. 3Com is focusing its initial efforts on providing policy-powered network solutions to support Class of Service (CoS) and Quality of Service (QoS), enhancing security capabilities, and automating systems management, such as device configuration, device monitoring, and address management.

When assessing PPN, we must identify the role of its directories. Also, a general model for policy transactions must be defined. When a policy transaction model is introduced, there must be a way to provide broad distribution of policy enforcement and inclusion of legacy devices. Proxies will play a major role in this process.

Directories are simple databases; they are not designed to collect information from multiple sources and then make a policy decision. The main difference between a directory configuration system and a policy-powered networking system is statefulness. In a simple directory configuration, a device pulls a static configuration from the central repository. In a policy-powered system, the directory still stores static information, but a policy server interprets this information in the context of other circumstantial data.

As shown in Figure 2.2, policy-powered systems offer greater flexibility and automation, as well as the ability for the network to offer differentiated, personalized service since the focus is on rules applied to users and groups, rather than configuration applied to devices.

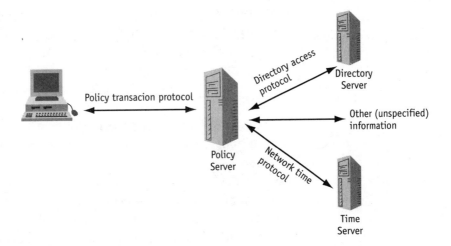

FIGURE 2.2   Policy-powered networking

In Figure 2.2, policy-powered networking employs a policy server that accesses information from multiple sources, collecting all relevant information, making policy decisions, and communicating these decisions to the network via a policy transaction protocol. This model reduces network administration while enhancing management control over a new generation of network applications. In this model, policy is essential for managing converged voice, video and data traffic across an ever-growing network infrastructure.

CIM's Contribution to DEN's Specification

The Common Information Model is the standard schema for managing desktop systems. CIM is also being developed by the DMTF. CIM describes manageable objects such as computer systems, network systems, and software packages. Directory service products like Active Directory describe users and the objects they use, such as files, applications, and printers.

When directory services have networking extensions, the gap between manageable objects and the users who require service from them is bridged. So this work is complementary to that of CIM, and network management tools will use both. CIM will be used mainly for equipment inventory purposes, and possibly to monitor, troubleshoot, and configure devices. Directory-enabling networks are part of a higher level of service that defines the relationships between networks, users, and network services.

A primary goal of CIM is the presentation of a consistent view of the managed environment independent of the various protocols and data formats supported by those devices and applications. CIM has gained acceptance by many network infrastructure and management software providers as an information model for enterprise management tools.

DEN and CIM have many common information needs. The DEN extended schema is primarily concerned with the expression and management of network element information in both enterprise and Internet Service Provider (ISP) networks. The DEN schema also addresses the network services and policies that control the provisioning of network elements. DEN's representation of network element information complements and enhances the existing network model of CIM. Its representation of network services and policies also extends the current version of CIM.

The DEN schema incorporates concepts from both X.500 and CIM. CIM promotes synergy between integrated, enhanced network and directory applications and management applications that use CIM:

✦ CIM defines several types of data, including management, device and system data. Some of this is appropriate for storing in the directory, and some is better suited for storing in other types of repositories. DEN will help enable other types of data stores to communicate better with directory-enabled applications. In addition, applications written to use CIM provide additional data that will expand and enhance DEN.

✦ The directory is a natural repository of information for CIM and applications written to use CIM.

✦ The DEN specification enhances CIM by providing a network model for representing network elements and services.

✦ The DEN specification extends CIM by adding models for defining and enforcing policy and network services.

✦ Network applications integrated with the directory benefit from CIM, and CIM-based applications benefit from network applications integrated with the directory, with minimal effort on the part of the application developer. This is because the directory-enabled network schema is an extension schema of CIM. Thus, there is no need for cumbersome information mapping.

CHAPTER 3

Defining the Directory-Enabled Network Schema

When defining DENs one must identify the applications, beginning by reviewing the appropriate use of directory services. Existing directory services provide schemas that define users and applications. The DEN schema defines network elements and services and how they interact with applications, users, and other services. This set of added functionality augments the existing capabilities of the directory. It also enables third-party independent software vendors (ISVs) and other application implementers to refine this set of base classes to provide their own application-specific functionality.

Understanding DEN[1]

DEN specification defines a schema and an information model for representing network element and service information and relationships gathered from the network using existing protocols and other sources of network information. An access protocol is also included to store and retrieve information.

The specification develops a robust directory service for storing network element and service information. It also defines an extensible information model representing the structural, behavioral and functional relationships between objects in the schema. Finally, LDAP access protocol is used to access, manage and manipulate directory information.

DEN Base Schema

The schema of a directory defines the set of objects that can be created in that directory and the set of attributes that can be used to describe those objects.

The DEN schema consists of abstract base classes from which all other network-specific classes are derived. The base classes are refined by specialization from the basic model for representing network elements, services, consumers, etc.

---

1 This section includes the collaboration of Xinzhong Yu (**xyu@cc.hut.fi**), from the Department of Computer Science and Engineering of Helsinki University of Technology.

When reviewing DEN's base schema and extension model we should consider:

✦ LDAP capabilities
✦ Syntax
✦ Base classes
✦ Class hierarchy
✦ Extension model.

The schema of a directory defines the set of objects that can be created in that directory and the set of attributes that can be used to describe those objects.

LDAP Capabilities

The Lightweight Directory Access Protocol (LDAP) version 3 defines a means for a client to view the schema of a directory. However, the LDAP does not define a schema, nor does it define how to extend a directory schema.

The definition of an object in a directory schema, called a *class*, will contain:

✦ The list of attributes that an instance of the class must have to be stored in the directory
✦ The list of additional attributes that an instance of the class may have
✦ The list of classes that can be parents of instances of the class
✦ The list of classes from which the class is derived.

The directory-enabled network schema can be implemented on any directory service that:

✦ Supports LDAP v3
✦ Provides an extensible schema
✦ Supports inheritance.

An Overview of LDAP

The LDAP was originally developed in the early 1990s to provide a light alternative to X.500 directory access protocol (DAP). It was designed to provide the most important functions of DAP, and simplify its implementation in servers and clients. LDAP was specifically designed for management and browser applications that require fundamental read/write access to directory services.

LDAP is an emerging software protocol for enabling anyone to locate organizations, individuals, and other resources such as files and devices in a network, whether on the Internet or on a corporate intranet. LDAP is lighter because in its initial version it did not include security features. The protocol has been endorsed by at least 40 companies. Netscape is including it in its latest Communicator suite of products. Microsoft plans to include it as part of its Exchange messaging product. Novell has announced that its Net-Ware Directory Services will interoperate with LDAP.

In a network, a directory tells where in the network something is located. On TCP/IP networks, including the Internet, the Domain Name System (DNS) is the directory system used to relate the domain name to a specific network address. LDAP permits searching for an individual without knowing the location.

LDAP directories are organized in a simple "tree" hierarchy, as shown in Figure 3.1 and consist of the following levels:

+ The "root" directory, which branches out to
+ Countries, each of which branches out to
+ Organizations, which branch out to
+ Organizational units (divisions, departments, and so forth), which branch out to
+ Individuals (which includes people, files, and shared resources such as printers).

An LDAP directory can be distributed among many servers. Each server can have a replicated version of the total directory that is synchronized periodically. An LDAP server is called a *Directory System Agent* (DSA). These servers are analogous to reference librarians in several libraries. Replication can be used to synchronize the listings between DSAs.

In addition, X.500 directories can be secured using public-key encryption and digital signatures. Each X.500 operation and result can be signed to preclude tampering. An LDAP server that receives a request from a user takes responsibility for the request, passing it to other DSAs as necessary, but ensuring a single coordinated response for the user.

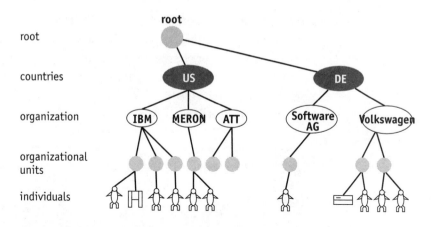

root

countries

organization

organizational
units

individuals

FIGURE 3.1   LDAP directories are organized in a simple tree hierarchy

One of the most important features of both X.500 and LDAP is the ability to search for user-specified resources. Note that this is completely different from the full-text searching prevalent on today's Web in engines like Excite or AltaVista. Directory searches are more like database queries than pattern-matching operations.

In becoming lightweight, LDAP sacrifices some of X.500's power. It makes up for this in four ways:

1. It was designed to run over TCP, making it ideal for Internet and intranet applications. X.500 DAP requires special networking software to access the wire.
2. It has simpler functions, making it easier and less expensive for vendors to implement.
3. It encodes its protocol elements in a less complex way than X.500, streamlining coding/decoding of requests.
4. Its servers take responsibility for referrals. X.500 DSAs return this information to the client, which must then issue a new search request. LDAP servers return only results, which lightens their burden and makes a sea of distributed X.500 servers appear as a single logical directory.

Syntax

The syntax of LDAP is defined as a subset of RFC 2252[2]. LDAP requires that the contents of AttributeValue fields in protocol elements be octet strings. A set of syntaxes is then necessary for LDAPv3 and the rules by which attribute values of these syntaxes are represented as octet strings for transmission in the LDAP protocol.

Figure 3.2 lists the components of LDAP syntax. More information about the syntaxes and attribute types is available in RFC 2252 at URL **http://andrew3.andrew.cmu.edu/rfc/rfc2253.html**.

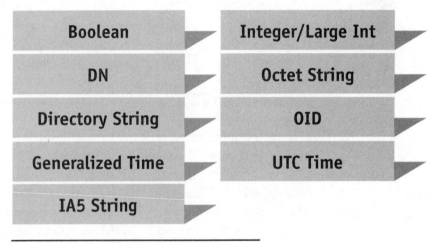

FIGURE 3.2   List of components of LDAP's syntax

All documents defining attribute syntax encoding for use with LDAP are expected to conform to RFC 2252 requirements. The encoding rules defined for a given attribute syntax must produce octet strings. To the greatest extent possible, encoded octet strings should be usable in their native encoded form for display purposes. In particular, encoding rules for attribute syntaxes defining non-binary values should produce strings that can be displayed with little or no translation by clients implementing LDAP. There are a few cases (e.g. multimedia) however, when it is not sensible to produce a printable representation, and clients MUST NOT assume that an unrecognized syntax is a string representation.

In encodings where an arbitrary string, not a distinguished name, is used as part of a larger production, and other than as part of a dis-

2 Network Working Group, Standards Track: M. Wahl, Critical Angle Inc.; A. Coulbeck, Isode Inc.; T. Howes, Netscape Communications Corp.; S. Kille, Isode Limited. – December 1997.

tinguished name, a backslash quoting mechanism is used to escape the following separator symbol character (such as "", "$" or "#") if it should occur in that string. A pair of hexadecimal digits representing the next character follows the backslash. A backslash itself in the string, which forms part of a larger syntax, is always transmitted as '\5C' or '\5c'.

Syntaxes are also defined for matching rules whose assertion value syntax is different from the attribute value syntax.

Base Classes

The DEN schema consists of abstract base classes from which all other network-specific classes are derived. The base classes are refined by specialization from the basic model for representing network elements, services, consumers, etc.

The base classes provide the building blocks for modeling the physical and logical structure of a network and its services, the consumers of those services and the rules for dispensing services to consumers.

Class Hierarchies

DEN is the aggregation of concepts from the currently released version of the CIM specification, the currently released version of the X.500 specification and a collection of new ideas. The new ideas build on the framework provided by CIM and X.500 in order to model network elements and services.

Figure 3.3 provides a view of the base class hierarchy. Note that the figure does not include most of infrastructure classes.

Extension Model

An *extension model* is a set of additional schema and information model definitions. The base schema is extended through the addition of new attributes and object classes, while the information model is extended through the addition of new relationships.

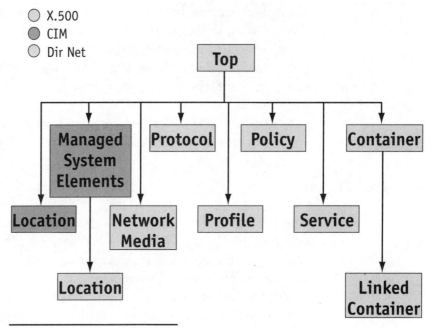

FIGURE 3.3 Base class hierarchy

An extension can assume many forms but only one is supported in the context of this specification:

✦ A new class is defined as a subclass of an existing class defined in the base schema. The extension defines any new attributes that apply to the new class and adds them to the list of "must have" or "may have" attributes for the new class. This approach is required by the specification in order to keep the class distinct.

Other methods of extending base classes are not allowed with the base classes defined in the specification. They are:

✦ Existing attributes that are added to existing classes defined in the base schema. In this case the attributes are already defined in the base schema; the extension adds selected attributes to the list of "must have" or "may have" attributes for an existing class.

✦ New attributes are defined and added to existing classes defined in the base schema. In this case the extension defines attributes and adds them to the list of "must have" or "may have" attributes for an existing class.

✦ An implementer can create any number of completely new objects using this method.

✦ A completely new class is defined (a subclass of "TOP", the class from which all classes derive).

Relationships can be either subclassed from existing relationships or defined as completely new entities. Although there are many forms of relationships that could be defined, this specification only defines associations and aggregations. This is in order to improve interoperability among differing implementations.

DEN Is Not Just a Schema

DEN is not just a schema, but also has an associated information model. The primary purpose of DEN is to separate the specification and representation of network elements and services from implementation details. Thus, DEN enables an ISP to specify that QoS should be applied to flows to a set of devices. DEN classes are used to provide this service specification to the appropriate set of devices without specifying how the various levels of QoS are actually implemented. This is because the actual mechanisms used to provide QoS are different for each vendor's device. DEN can be used to determine which devices should be provisioned and where they are located.

A secondary purpose of DEN is to provide a framework that can be extended by vendor-specific subclasses to represent vendor-specific functionality and implementation mechanisms. DEN's class hierarchy and information model is necessarily general in nature, consisting mostly of base classes that enable this subclassing to be done.

The CIM provides a rich framework for the information model, including representation of products, systems, applications, and components that can be managed. In addition, CIM provides a reasonably complete definition of an application, including modeling the various states that an application can take.

Description

The information model is composed of a set of base classes providing a general framework with specific class hierarchies that model network elements and services, applications, and end-users. It can be used as a repository to define how objects are to be built and relate to each other, as well as to define a common meta-schema. In addition, it can be used as a means to build applications and exchange information. In doing so, it can define how the information is stored and establish a common name space and mapping using common protocols, as well as common object models. Figure 3.4 provides an overview of the information model.

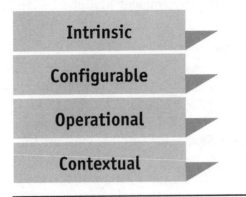

FIGURE 3.4   Object model type of information

An object model describes the static and structural aspects of objects in system, which includes these types of information: intrinsic, configuration, operational, and contextual.

This framework defines the application-specific behavior and needs. The objective of the information model is to preset a set of consistent views of the environment being managed. These views should be extensible, to enable application-specific needs to be accommodated, as well as independent of protocols and data format being used. In addition, the framework should have a common way of defining and manipulating common sets of objects.

Common Information Model

CIM provides a framework, including representation of products, systems, applications, and components that can be managed. It also provides a definition of an application, which includes modeling the various states that an application can take. These concepts as defined by CIM are sufficient for supporting the initial development of network element and services modeling as defined in this version of the DEN specification.

The X.500 specification proposes basic definitions to represent person and application. Both provide fundamental concepts in the directory service environment, and augment the ideas expressed in CIM. The DEN specification augments the definitions of the Person and Device classes to enable them to be used to describe and control the interaction among users, applications, network elements and services. DEN will assume an X.500-based model of person and application to use in developing the representation of network elements and services and their binding to users and applications.

This information model provides a strategy for application developers using a common framework to enable disparate applications to share a common name space and schema, along with common rules to govern how those objects interact with other objects, to be used by heterogeneous applications. Thus, applications with completely different purposes but operating on common objects can exchange information and knowledge about those objects.

Therefore, if an ISV develops an application which populates the schema with information describing the characteristics of the network, another ISV can use this application in conjunction with another application to provision a network, while a third application from a third vendor could be used to manage devices in the network. Furthermore, due to its object-oriented nature, information could be shared and reused by each of these applications, providing a great degree of interoperability. Note that at the time of this writing, Fall 1998, such features are not present in the specification but are part of the workgroup's goal.

Application-specific needs are accommodated by refining the DEN classes into more specific subclasses to represent the desired additional functionality. This refines the framework while keeping a common schema and relationships. New subclasses inherit the attributes of their parent, and can include whatever additional attributes are necessary. A characteristic of inheritance is that an instance of a subclass is also an instance of all the parent classes from which it inherits.

The interaction of users and applications with the network elements and services, and the management of network elements and services, are defined by the information model. The information model is a robust object-oriented model that defines the behavior of and interaction between network elements and services, and users and applications.

Relationships are expressed via containment, which is used to assemble a collection of parts into a whole by expressing the collection as a hierarchy of containers. For example, a router might consist of a chassis, which contains slots, each of which contains networkcards, and so on. Reference is used to express peer relationships between objects.

An attribute of a given Connector object might contain a reference to the Media object to which that connector is attached. Note that relationships can also express dependencies between objects. For example, aggregation often implies (but does not require) that the aggregated objects have mutual dependencies.

An Overview of DEN's Information Model

As discussed in Chapter 1, the purpose of integrating directory services and the network is to provide an environment in which the information published in the directory can be leveraged by applications to provide enhanced functionality and services. This is done by having all the applications interacting with each other via an integrated information model.

This information model is characterized as an abstraction of knowledge so that it can be understood before implementation. The model structures the knowledge about users, applications, networks, and how they interact into multiple knowledge domains to enable different people to use it. This structuring is done using uniform object-oriented (OO) modeling to support the cooperative development of an OO schema and an information model.

The information model consists of three parts:

+ Six base class hierarchies that form the basic framework that represents network elements and services
+ An extensible schema based on inheritance and aggregation for modeling application-specific properties and information
+ Simple mechanisms for establishing relationships among object instances.

The primary purpose of DEN is to separate the specification and representation of network elements and services from implementation details. A secondary purpose is to provide an extensible framework to represent vendor-specific functionality and implementation mechanisms by vendor-specific subclasses.

As shown in Figure 3.5, this information model should describe the relationships among objects in tasks such as:

✦ Controlling how distinct objects interact with each other, either by binding users to network services or by enforcing a policy

✦ Remaining independent of any particular implementation to enable the exchange of information among different domains and to help the interoperability of applications.

• Controls the distinction of object interactions with each other, binding users to network services or enforcing a policy.

• Is always independent to specific implementations to enable interoperability of applications and exchange of information across heterogeneous platforms and domains.

FIGURE 3.5 Information model definition

The network elements and services form six base class hierarchies:

1. Network Device
2. Network Protocol
3. Network Media
4. Network Service
5. Profile
6. Policy.

The Common Information Model and X.500

The DEN schema incorporates concepts from both CIM and X.500.

The CIM, as briefly discussed in Chapter 1, is an object-oriented conceptual model for the information required to manage many common aspects of complex computer systems defined by the

DMTF. CIM provides a rich framework, including representation of products, systems, applications, and components that can be managed. The concepts defined by CIM are used for supporting the network element and services modeling in DEN.

X.500 is the name given to a series of standards developed by the International Organization for Standardization/International Telecommunication Union–Telecommunication Standardization Center (ISO/ITU-T) that specify how information can be stored and accessed in a global directory service. The X.500 specification proposes basic definitions to represent person and application. DEN will assume an X.500-based model of person and application to use in developing the representation of network elements and services and their binding to users and applications.

A Review of the X.500 Global Directory Service

As a standard, X.500 enables the development of an electronic directory of people in an organization so that it can be part of a global directory available to anyone with Internet access. Such a directory is sometimes called a *global white pages directory*, as it enables the lookup of people in a user-friendly way by name, department, or organization. Many companies already use the X.500 directory. Because these directories are organized as part of a single global directory, it is possible to search for hundreds of thousands of people from a single place on the Web.

The X.500 directory is organized under a common "root" directory in a tree hierarchy of country, organization, or corporate departments and person. An entry at each of these levels must have certain attributes; some of these can be optional ones established locally. Each organization can implement a directory in its own way as long as it adheres to the basic schema or plan. The distributed global directory works through a registration process and one or more central places that manage many directories.

TIP

In computer programming, a schema is the organization or structure for a database. The activity of *data modeling* leads to a schema. The plural form is *schemata*. The term is used in discussing both relational and object-oriented databases.

The use of the X.500 directory allows an organization to make itself and selected members known on the Internet. Two of the largest directory service providers are InterNIC, the organization that supervises domain name registration in the U.S., and ESNet, which maintains X.500 data for all the U.S. national laboratories. ESNet and similar providers also provide access to looking up names in the global directory, using a number of different user interfaces including designated Web sites, whois, and finger. These organizations also provide assistance to organizations creating their own DITs.

In X.500, each local directory is called a *Directory System Agent* (DSA). A DSA can represent one organization or a group of organizations. The DSAs are interconnected from the DIT. The user interface program for access to one or more DSAs is a Directory User Agent (DUA). DUAs include whois, finger, and programs that offer a graphical user interface. X.500 is implemented as part of the Distributed Computing Environment (DCE) in its Global Directory Service (GDS). The University of Michigan is one of a number of universities that use X.500 as a way to route e-mail and provide name lookup, using LDAP.

X.500 Components

X.500 defines a complex and heavyweight set of standards as listed in Figure 3.6. These standards address the following components:

- ✦ The hierarchical name space, which determines how information is referenced and organized
- ✦ The information model, describing the format and the structure of information maintained in the directory
- ✦ The functional model, specifying the directory access protocol and specific operations, such as read, write, search and authenticate, that may be performed on the information residing in the directory
- ✦ The authentication model, protecting the information stored in the directory from unauthorized access or modification
- ✦ The distributed operation model, determining how data are distributed and the operations that must be performed to synchronize and maintain the global directory across thousands of servers.

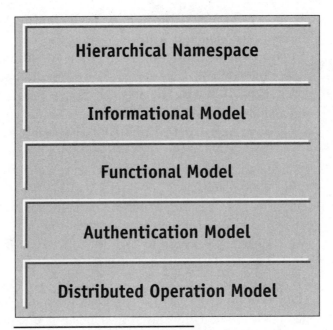

FIGURE 3.6   X.500 set of standards

X.500's six base class hierarchies define the root for DEN's representation of network elements and services composing the information model. These are listed in Figure 3.7:

✦ Network Device
✦ Network Protocol
✦ Network Media
✦ Profile
✦ Policy
✦ Network Service

The X.500 six base-class hierarchies form the root for DEN's representation of network elements and services. Refining the DEN classes into more specific subclasses to represent the desired additional functionality accommodates application-specific needs.

The meta-schema defines the schema based on object definitions, aggregation and constraint. As Figure 3.8 shows, the information model uses:

✦ Repository, by defining how objects are built and relate to each other, as well as in the common meta-schema

✦ Application builder and means of information exchange, by defining storage and formatting (using common protocols) for information and a common object model.

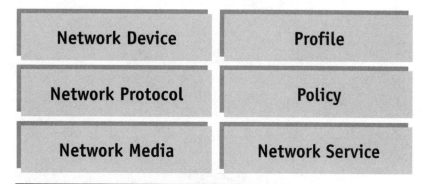

Network Device	Profile
Network Protocol	Policy
Network Media	Network Service

FIGURE 3.7   X.500 six base class hierarchies

• Repository, by defining how objects are built and relate to each other, as well as common meta-schema.

• Application builder and means of information exchanged, by defining storage and formatting (using common protocols) for information and a common object model.

FIGURE 3.8   Information model uses

Exchanging Model Information

Once network elements are bootstrapped into the system, they will exchange a set of queries and responses with information about themselves. Four different types of information, outlined in Figure 3.9, are necessary to model the structural information of network elements and services:

✦ **Intrinsic:** Information essential to representing a particular element or service

✦ **Configurable:** Information that controls the operation of a device, or helps determine how that device or service operates

+ **Operational:** Information that controls how a device or service interacts with its surrounding environment
+ **Contextual:** Information defining how the device or service relates to other components in a larger, network-wide context.

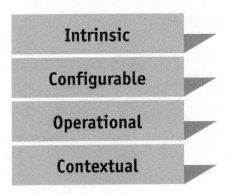

FIGURE 3.9 The four different types of information necessary to model the structural information of network elements and services

DEN's Relationship Models

The DEN information model consists of a data model and a relationship model. The schema represents the data model. The relationship model describes how different objects in the schema are related to one another.

The three main types of relationships, are shown in Figure 3.10:

+ **Links:** Physical or conceptual relationships between object instances. The relationship can be defined as an ordered double. A link is an instance of an association. If the multiplicity of the association can change, it should be modeled as a class. If links can participate in associations, then the associations should be modeled as class.
+ **Associations** (shown in Figure 3.11): A group of links with a common structure and set of semantics. An association can be modeled as a class with its own attributes and methods.
+ **Aggregations:** A special type of association. An aggregation has a strong form of association in which an aggregate object is composed of components. It represents a relationship in which some

objects are "a-part-of" another object. Aggregation has additional semantics, such as transitivity (a ➔ b, b ➔ c, then a ➔), anti-symmetricity (if a is part of b, then b is not part of a), separability, and property propagation.

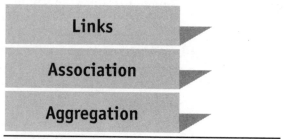

FIGURE 3.10 DEN's main types of relationship models

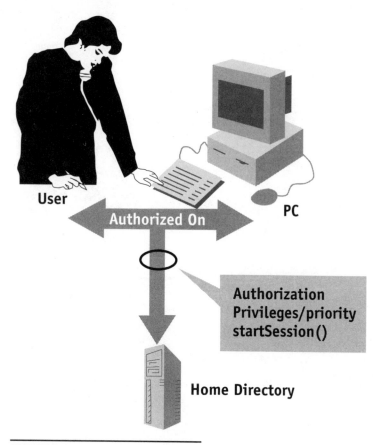

FIGURE 3.11 Example of association

A Word About Multiplicity

Multiplicity specifies how many instances of one class may relate to a single instance of an associated class. It may be expressed in intervals or sets, but it will always depend on how the boundaries of a problem are defined. It exposes hidden assumptions built into the model.

CHAPTER **4**

The DMTF Common Information Model (CIM)

As defined by the Desktop Management Task Force (DMTF), the CIM is a common data model of an implementation-neutral schema for describing overall management information in a network/enterprise environment. CIM is comprised of a specification and a schema. The specification defines the details for integration with other management models while the schema provides the actual model descriptions.

What Is CIM?

CIM is an object-oriented conceptual model for the information required to manage many common aspects of complex computer systems defined by the DMTF. CIM is under ongoing development, part of an industry initiative for enabling enterprise management of devices and applications.

CIM enables accessing management data completely interoperable among management applications, including configuration, performance and change management. Think of CIM as Simple Network Management Protocol (SNMP) on steroids. CIM enables correlation between management applications and heterogeneous management objects. Although I still am not sure how CIM (and DEN for that matter) will affect network and systems management, I can clearly see the promises it makes for better root-cause analysis and control of more network objects from a single management platform.

NOTE

SNMP governs network management and the monitoring of network devices and their functions. It is not necessarily limited to TCP/IP networks. Additional information on SNMP is available in the Internet Engineering Task Force (IETF) RFC 1089–SNMP over Ethernet.

CIM's major goal is the presentation of a consistent view of the managed environment independent of the various protocols and data formats supported by those devices and applications. It has gained acceptance by many network infrastructure and management software providers as an information model for enterprise management tools since it promises both to enable end-to-end application management and protect the installed base of SNMP, DMI, Common Management Information Protocol (CMIP) and proprietary management bases.

To achieve end-to-end management, CIM establishes the way managed objects connect to the network and systems, and where they sit in relation to other objects managed on the network and systems. For instance, a managed desktop running a client/server application can be tracked not only for its version and the environment in which it runs on a user's PC, but also by where it sits on the network and the path and infrastructure it must traverse to reach the server application.

The most interesting thing is that these relationships, while mapped by CIM, hold no special intelligence; this forces CIM applications to understand what to do with the managed data, even though the applications will be easier to define and offer a richer content.

Therefore, CIM targets the management of systems and networks that apply the basic structuring and conceptualization techniques of the object-oriented paradigm. The approach uses a uniform modeling formalism that—together with the basic repertoire of object-oriented constructs—supports the cooperative development of an object-oriented schema across multiple organizations.

A management schema and information model that uses Untried Modeling Language (UML) to manage systems is provided to establish a common conceptual framework at the level of a fundamental typology. With respect to classification and association, and with respect to a basic set of classes, this is intended to establish a common framework for a description of the managed environment. The management schema is divided into these conceptual layers:

✦ **Core model:** An information model that captures notions applicable to all areas of management. The core model is a small set of classes, associations and properties providing a basic vocabulary for analyzing and describing managed systems. It represents a starting point for the analyst in determining how to extend the common schema. Although additional classes may be added to the core model later on, major reinterpretations of its classes are not anticipated.

✦ **Common model:** An information model that captures notions common to particular management areas, but independent of a particular technology or implementation. The common areas are systems, applications, databases, networks and devices. The common model is a basic set of classes that define various technology-independent areas: systems, applications, networks, and devices.

The classes, properties, associations and methods in the common model provide a view of the area detailed enough to use as a basis for program design and even implementation. Extensions are added below the common model in platform-specific additions that supply concrete classes and implementations of the common model classes. As the common model is extended, it will offer a broader range of information.

◆ **Extension schemata:** These represent technology-specific extensions of the common model. They are specific to environments, such as operating systems (for example, UNIX or Microsoft Windows).

The extension schemata are technology-specific extensions to the common model, which should evolve as a result of the promotion of objects and properties defined in the extension schemata.

Generally, information used to perform tasks is organized or structured to allow disparate groups of people to use it. This can be accomplished by developing a model or representation of the details required by people working within a particular domain. Such an approach can be referred to as an information model.

The information model provides the basis for the development of management applications. The common model provides a set of base classes for extension into the area of technology-specific schemata. The core and common models together are expressed as the CIM schema.

An information model requires a set of legal statement types (syntax) to capture the representation, and a collection of actual expressions necessary to manage common aspects of the domain.

Further development work on CIM is planned by the DMTF CIM Technical Development Committee. Up-to-date information on this work may be found at their Web site: **http://www.dmtf.org/work/cim.html**.

TIP

CIM's objective is to manage individual components in the context of the enterprise. Thus, both DEN and CIM have common information needs. The schema for network integration defined here was based on the extension schema version 2.0 of CIM, the one available at the time of this writing. Keep in mind that DEN is still under development. In any case, the DEN extended schema is primarily concerned with the expression and management of network element information in both enterprise and Service Provider networks, but network services and policies that control the provisioning of network elements are still addressed by the DEN schema.

The representation of a network element information DEN elaborates complements and enhances the existing network model of CIM while DEN's representation of network services and policies extends CIM's current version. In addition, as discussed in Chapter 1, DEN's schema incorporates concepts from both X.500 and CIM. CIM, in particular, promotes synergy between integrated, enhanced network and directory applications and management applications that use CIM since:

◆ CIM defines several types of data, such as management, device and system data
◆ The directory is a natural repository of information for CIM and applications written to use CIM
◆ The DEN specification enhances CIM. It provides a network model for representing network elements and services
◆ The DEN specification extends CIM by adding models for defining and enforcing policy and network services
◆ Network applications integrated with the directory benefit from CIM, and CIM-based applications benefit from network applications integrated with the directory. This occurs without requiring any additional efforts from the application's developer.

The two-way benefits provided by network applications integrated with the directory from CIM are possible because the DEN schema is an extension schema of CIM; this obviates the need for complicated and odd information mapping.

Note that some of the data types defined by CIM are appropriate for storing in the directory, and some are better suited for storing in other types of repositories. DEN can help enable other types of data stores to communicate better with directory-enabled applications. In addition, applications written to use CIM provide additional data that will expand and enhance DEN.

Management Challenge

Today's network environment is heterogeneous and almost impossible to manage and control. Customers are placed in a distributed environment where, as Sun Microsystems would define, "the network is the computer." Users have access to a variety of resources at their intranets and extended through the extranets. Resources can vary from printing and file services through access information and applications across the network.

As depicted in Figure 4.1, today's environment emphasizes the customer's concern with the applications he or she runs and availability, since mid-level servers are distributed not only in a LAN, but also across metropolitan area networks (MANs) and WANs, crossing public networks, and therefore making it difficult to have QoS guarantees.

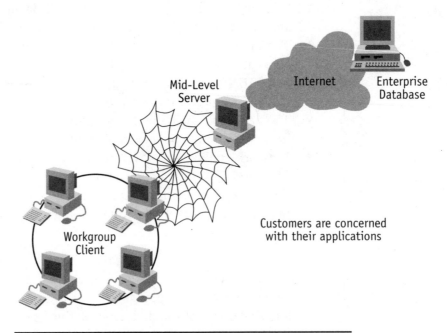

FIGURE 4.1   Typical client/server distributed network environment

The CIM proposition targets today's client/server distributed networking challenges, which can be divided in four main layers, as depicted in Figure 4.2:

   ✦ Physical managed objects
   ✦ Service layer and infrastructure
   ✦ Managed resource definition
   ✦ Management application.

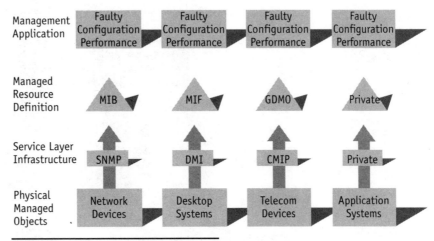

FIGURE 4.2 CIM management challenge

As Figure 4.2 describes, the physical layer challenges revolve around network devices, desktop systems, telecommunication devices and application systems. These physical objects are usually managed by a variety of tools. Typically we use SNMP for network device management. Desktop systems use the desktop management interface (DMI), an industry interface, for keeping track of and monitoring the status of components in a system of desktop personal computers.

DMTF created the DMI. Each component in a PC system must provide a Management Information File (MIF) that describes its characteristics. Intel's LANDesk Client Manager (LDCM) is based on DMI. Dell Computers plans to offer DMI support in its NetPCs as part of a Total Cost of Ownership (TCO) strategy. Figure 4.3 provides a schema of Sun Microsystems' view of DMI.

As for telecommunication devices, the service layer usually defined relies on the Common Management Information Protocol (CMIP), a network management protocol built on the Open Systems Interconnection (OSI) communication model. The related Common Management Information Services (CMIS) defines services for accessing information about network objects or devices, controlling them, and receiving status reports from them. Application systems generally use proprietary services for management and monitoring.

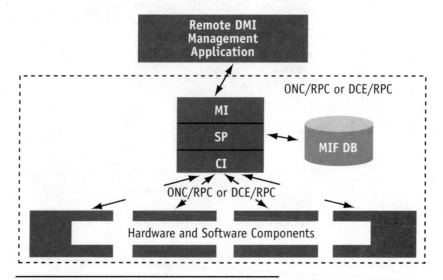

FIGURE 4.3 DMI diagram. *Source: Sun Microsystems*

Despite the many platforms and environments in existence today, corporations and their IT organizations still want to be able to manage their software and applications in an "end to end" fashion. Of course, they want to achieve this style of management in the most automated, secure, and "hands-off" method possible. IT groups also want to be able to promise and deliver on committed levels of service, both to minimize the overall costs of managing platforms and to minimize the impact of platform management on the people who need these managed systems to do their jobs. This is the main challenge CIM targets.

In order for CIM to be successful, it must be transparent. IT organizations have spent a great deal of effort in building information to help manage networks, servers, and client platforms. Any new components introduced into the overall management scheme must protect and preserve the existing investments in management information. CIM must help IT managers at a central location manage and

integrate a wide assortment of heterogeneous management components, managed platforms, and managed systems. Figure 4.4 depicts
CIM's proposition to integrate and at the same time overlap the information and tools being used today to manage network resources.

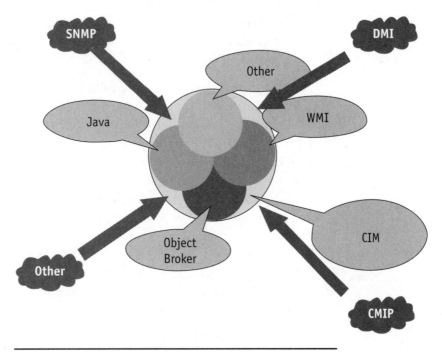

FIGURE 4.4   CIM works as a catalyst for platform manageability

NOTE

Microsoft is using the term *Windows Management Instrumentation* (WMI) to
describe how Microsoft implements WBEM for Windows. It is fully compliant with
the DMTF CIM and Web-based Enterprise Management (WBEM) specifications.
WMI is now used by Microsoft where the terms "WBEM" and "WBEM for Windows" were used previously, and WMI will continue to conform to future DMTF
WBEM specifications.

CIM at Work: What to Expect

Much is expected from CIM. As an implementation-neutral schema
(better yet, data model) for describing overall management information, CIM:

✦ Facilitates the common understanding of management data across different management systems
✦ Facilitates management information integration from different sources
✦ Is a data model, which should not be confused with an implementation
✦ Provides models for both instrumentation and management
✦ Is not WBEM, which is an implementation of CIM.

As a data model, CIM will initially be used to model management information from desktops and servers. It will be used to describe management information between differing management application such as TME10, HP's OpenView, Microsoft's SMS and so forth, to provide a common understanding of management information. Although previous attempts to accomplish this have not been successful, with the support of the industry the chances are much greater.

Customers should expect an impact from CIM since it will enable common description for all management data across all views, and the integration of data from different sources. As shown in Figure 4.4, CIM does not replace SNMP, DMI, etc. Rather, it enables IT groups to preserve their investment. In addition, CIM enables end-to-end management, such as for application management, and allows customers to concentrate on delivering service, thus lowering cost.

CIM Management Schema

Management schemata are the cornerstone for management of platforms and applications, including device configuration, performance management, and change management. In CIM, the managed environment is seen as a collection of interrelated systems composed of a number of discrete elements.

CIM supplies a set of classes with properties and associations that provide a conceptual framework to enable the organization of the available information about the managed environment. The expectation is that any programmer required to write code that will operate against the object schema, or any schema designer intending to make new information available within the managed environment, will clearly understand CIM.

CIM Implementations

CIM is a conceptual model that is not bound to a particular implementation. This allows it to be used to exchange management information in a variety of ways; four of these ways are illustrated in Figure 4.5. It is possible to use these ways in combination within a management application.

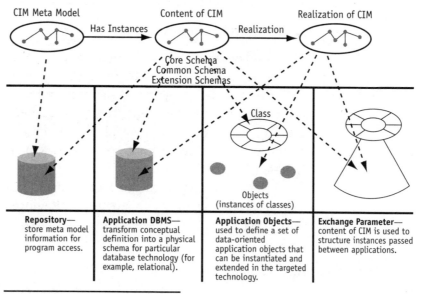

FIGURE 4.5 Four ways to use CIM

As Figure 4.5 shows, CIM can be used as a repository. The constructs defined in the model are stored in a database, but are not instances of the object, relationship, and so on. Rather they are definitions to be used in the establishment of objects and relationships. The meta-model used by CIM is stored in a repository that becomes a representation of the meta-model. This is accomplished by mapping the meta-model constructs into the physical schema of the targeted repository, then populating the repository with the classes and properties expressed in the CIM conceptual layers.

For an application DBMS, the CIM is mapped into the physical schema of a targeted DBMS, whereas the information stored consists of actual instances of the constructs. Applications can exchange information when they have access to a common DBMS and the mapping occurs in a predictable way.

The CIM is used to create a set of application objects in a particular language. Applications can exchange information when they can bind to the application objects. In the case of parameters, for example, the CIM is a neutral form used to exchange management information by way of a standard set of object APIs. Exchanges can be accomplished via a direct set of API calls or by exchange-oriented APIs, which can create the appropriate object in the local implementation technology.

Implementation Conformance

It is fundamental to CIM for information to be exchanged between management applications. CIM uses the Management Object Format (MOF) for exchanging management information. As of Fall 1998, no programming interfaces or protocols are defined by an exchange mechanism. Thus, a CIM-capable system must be able to import and export properly formed MOF constructs, which it does through compatible implementations.

Objects instantiated in the MOF must include all key properties and all properties marked as required. Required properties have the REQUIRED qualifier present and set to TRUE.

Expressing the Schemas

The meta-schema is a formal definition of the model and defines the terms used to express the model and its usage and semantics. The Unified Modeling Language (UML) is used to define the structure of the meta-schema.

NOTE

To fully understand meta-schemata one should be familiar with UML notation and with basic object-oriented concepts in the form of classes, properties, methods, operations, inheritance, associations, objects, cardinality, and polymorphism. For more information on UML check **http://www.rational.com/uml**.

Defining the Meta-Schema

The elements of the model, which also supports indications and associations as types of classes and references as types of properties, are:

+ **Schemata:** A group of classes with a single owner, used for administration and class naming. Class names must be unique within their owning schemata.

+ **Classes:** A collection of instances that support the same type (or the same properties and methods). They can be arranged in a generalization hierarchy that represents subtype relationships between classes. The generalization hierarchy is a rooted, directed graph and does not support multiple inheritance.

   Classes can have methods, which represent the behavior relevant for any class. A class may participate in associations by being the target of one of the references owned by the association. Note that classes also have instances.

+ **Properties:** A value used to characterize instances of a class. A property can be thought of as a pair of Get and Set functions that, when applied to an object, return state and set state, respectively.

+ **Methods:** A declaration of a signature, which in the case of a concrete class may imply an implementation.

TIP

An *indication* is an object created as a result of a trigger.

An *association* is a class that contains two or more references. It represents a relationship between two or more objects. Associations have no significance except that they can have references and be subclasses of non-association classes. Thus, any subclass of an association is an association.

References define the role each object plays in an association. The reference represents the role name of a class in the context of an association. Associations support the provision of multiple relationship instances for a given object.

Properties and methods have reflexive associations that represent property and method overriding. A method can override an inherited method. A similar interpretation implies the overriding of properties.

Qualifiers are used to characterize named elements. They provide a mechanism that makes the meta-schema extensible in a limited and controlled fashion. New types of qualifiers can be introduced by a new Qualifier name, providing new types of meta-data to processes that manage and manipulate classes, properties, and other elements of the meta-schema, as shown in Figure 4.6.

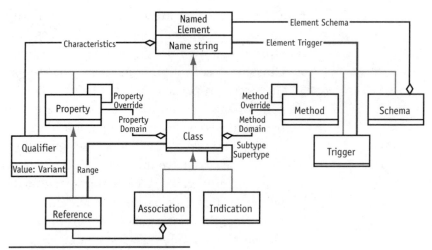

FIGURE 4.6   Meta-schema structure

Figure 4.6 provides an overview of the structure of the meta-schema. The rules defining the meta-schema are:

1. Every meta construct is expressed as a descendent of a named element.
2. A named element has zero or more characteristics (a qualifier that characterizes a named element).
3. A named element can trigger zero or more indications.
4. A schema is a named element and can contain zero or more classes, which must belong to only one schema.
5. A qualifier type is a named element and must be used to supply a type for a qualifier.
6. A qualifier is a named element and has a name, a type, a value of this type, a scope, a flavor, and a default value. The type of the Qualifier value must agree with the type of the Qualifier type.
7. A property is a named element and has only one domain: the class that owns the property.
8. A property can have an override relationship with another property from a different class. The domain of the overridden property must be a supertype of the domain of the overriding property.
9. The class referenced by the range association (shown in Figure 4.7), of an overriding reference must be the same as, or a subtype of, the class referenced by the range associations of the reference being overridden.

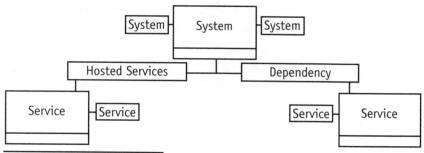

FIGURE 4.7 Reference naming

10. The domain of a reference must be an association.
11. A class is a type of named element. A class can have instances and is the domain for zero or more properties. A class is the domain for zero or more methods.
12. A class can have zero or one supertype, and zero or more subtypes.
13. An association is a type of class. Associations are classes with an association qualifier.
14. An association must have two or more references.
15. An association can inherit from a non-association class.
16. Any subclass of an association is an association.
17. A method is a named element and has only one domain: the class that owns the method.
18. A method can have an override relationship with another method from a different class. The domain of the overridden method must be a superclass of the domain of the overriding method.
19. A trigger is an operation that is invoked on any state change, such as object creation, deletion, modification or access, or on property modification or access. Qualifiers, qualifier types and schemas may not have triggers. The changes that invoke a trigger are specified as qualifiers.
20. An indication is a type of class and has an association with zero or more named triggers that can create instances of the indication.
21. Every meta-schema object is a descendent of a named element and, as such, has a name. All names are case-insensitive. The rules applicable to name vary, depending on the creation type of the object.

22. Qualifiers are characteristics of named elements which have a name (inherited from named element) and a value. The value is used to define the characteristics of the named element. A reference has a range that represents the type of the reference, as shown in Figure 4.8.

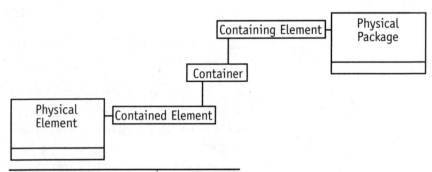

FIGURE 4.8   References, ranges, and domains

23. A class has a subtype-supertype association that represents substitutability relationships between the named elements involved in the relationship. The association implies that any instance of a subtype can be substituted for any instance of the supertype in an expression, without invalidating the expression, as shown in Figure 4.9.

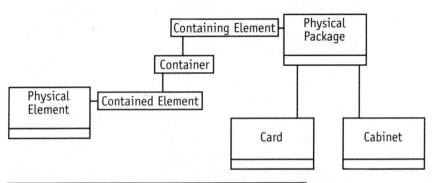

FIGURE 4.9   References, ranges, domains, and inheritances

Property Data Types

Property data types are limited to the intrinsic data types or arrays. Structured types are constructed by designing new classes. If the property is an array property, the corresponding variant type is simply the array equivalent of the variant for the underlying intrinsic type. Table 4.1 lists the intrinsic data types and their interpretation.

TABLE 4.1   The intrinsic data types and interpretations

Intrinsic Data Type	Interpretation
uint8	Unsigned 8-bit integer
sint8	Signed 8-bit integer
uint16	Unsigned 16-bit integer
sint16	Signed 16-bit integer
uint32	Unsigned 32-bit integer
sint32	Signed 32-bit integer
uint64	Unsigned 64-bit integer
sint64	Signed 64-bit integer
string	UCS-2 string
boolean	Boolean
real32	IEEE 4-byte floating-point
real64	IEEE 8-byte floating-point
datetime	A string containing a date-time
<classname> ref	Strongly typed reference
char16	16-bit UCS-2 character

Date, Time, and Interval Types

Date, datetime, interval, and time property types are aliases for each other and use the same fixed string-based format:

```
yyyymmddhhmmss.mmmmmmsuct
```

where

+ yyyy is a 4 digit year
+ mm is the month
+ dd is the day
+ hh is the hour (24-hour clock)
+ mm is the minute
+ ss is the second
+ mmmmmm is the number of microseconds

✦ s is a "+" or "–", indicating the sign of the UCT (Universal Coordinated Time; for all intents and purposes the same as Greenwich Mean Time) correction field, or a ":". In this case, the value is interpreted as a time interval, and yyyymm are interpreted as days.

✦ uct is the offset from UCT in minutes (using the sign indicated by s). It is ignored for a time interval.

Supported Schema Modifications

Use of some supported schema modifications will result in changes in application behavior. Changes are all subject to security restrictions; in particular, only the owner of the schema, or someone authorized by the owner, can make modifications to the schema.

1. A class can be added to or deleted from a schema.
2. A property can be added to or deleted from a class.
3. A class can be added as a subtype or supertype of an existing class.
4. A class can become an association as a result of the addition of an association qualifier, plus two or more references.
5. A qualifier can be added to or deleted from any named element.
6. The override qualifier can be added to or removed from a property or reference.
7. A class can alias a property (or reference, if the class is a descendent of an association), using the alias qualifier. Both inherited and immediate properties of the class may be aliased.
8. A method can be added to a class.
9. A method can override an inherited method.
10. Methods can be deleted, and the signature of a method can be changed.
11. A trigger may be added to or deleted from a class.

In defining an extension to a schema, the schema designer is expected to operate within the constraints of the classes defined in the core model. Once the core model class to be extended is identified, each of the subclasses of the identified class should be treated the same way. This process, which defines the superclasses of the class to be defined, should be continued until the most detailed class is identified. The core model is not a part of the meta-schema, but is an important device for introducing uniformity across schemata intended to represent aspects of the managed environment.

Being Aware of Schema Versions

Schema modifications can cause failure in applications that operated against the schema prior to the modification. These modifications are:

◆ Deletion of classes, properties, or methods
◆ Movements of a class anywhere other than down a hierarchy
◆ Alteration of property type or method signature
◆ Altering a reference range to anything other than the original specification.

Other alterations are considered to be interface-preserving. Any use of the schema changes listed above implies the generation of a new major version of the schema.

Specifications

Since CIM is not bound to a particular technology or implementation, sharing management information between a variety of management platforms should be facilitated. The CIM naming mechanism was defined to address enterprise-wide identification of objects, as well as the sharing of management information.

CIM naming addresses these requirements:

◆ Ability to locate and uniquely identify any object in an enterprise
  ✧ Unambiguous enumeration of all objects
  ✧ Ability to determine when two object names reference the same entity
  ✧ Location transparency (no need to understand which management platforms proxy other platforms' instrumentation)
◆ Allowing sharing of objects and instance data among management platforms
  ✧ Allowing creation of different scoping hierarchies which vary by "time" (for example, a "current" vs. "proposed" scoping hierarchy)

✦ Facilitating move operations between object trees (including within a single management platform)

◆ Hiding underlying management technology/provide technology transparency for the domain-mapping environment

◆ Making the object name identifiable regardless of instrumentation technology

◆ Allowing different names for DMI vs. SNMP objects; thus requires the management platform to understand how the underlying objects are implemented.

The key qualifier is the CIM meta-model mechanism used to identify the properties that uniquely identify an instance of a class, as shown in Figure 4.10. CIM naming enhances this base capability by:

✦ Introducing the weak and propagated qualifiers to express situations in which the keys of one object are to be propagated to another object

✦ Introducing the Source pragma and qualifier ("namespace-type://namespace_handle") to allow details about the implementation source to be recorded in an MOF file

✦ Introducing the NonLocal qualifier ("namespacetype://name-space_handle") to reference an object instance kept in another implementation.

MOF files can be used to populate a technology that understands the semantics and structure of CIM. When an MOF file is consumed by a particular implementation, there are two operations being performed, depending on the file's content. First, a compile or definition operation is performed to establish the structure of the model. Second, an import operation is performed to insert instances into the platform or tool.

Once the compile and import are completed, the actual instances are manipulated using the native capabilities of the platform or tool. The contents of a MOF file are loaded into a namespace that provides a domain (in other words, a container), in which the instances of the classes are guaranteed to be unique per the key qualifier definitions. The term namespace is used to refer to an implementation that provides such a domain.

Namespaces can be used to:

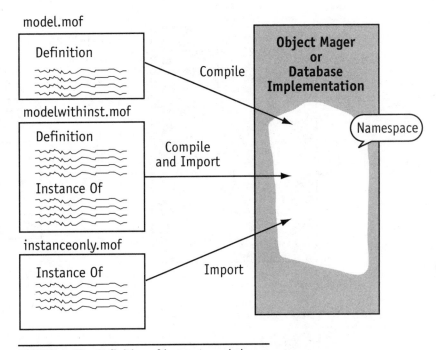

FIGURE 4.10   Definition of instances and classes

+ Define chunks of management information (objects and associations) to limit implementation resource requirements, such as database size
+ Define views on the model for applications managing only specific objects, such as hubs
+ Pre-structure groups of objects for optimized query speed.

Another viable operation is exporting from a particular management platform, as shown in Figure 4.11. Essentially, this operation creates an MOF file for all or some portion of the information content of a platform.

For example, information is exchanged when the source system is of type Mgmt_X and its name is EastCoast, as depicted in Figure 4.12. The export produces an MOF file with the circle and triangle definitions and instances 1, 3, and 5 of the circle class and instances 2 and 4 of the triangle class. This MOF file is then compiled and imported into the management platform of type Mgmt_ABC with the name AllCoasts.

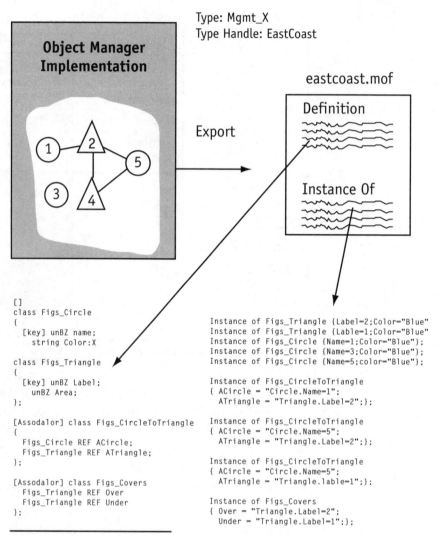

Type: Mgmt_X
Type Handle: EastCoast

eastcoast.mof

Object Manager Implementation

Definition

Instance Of

Export

```
[]
class Figs_Circle
{
  [key] unBZ name;
     string Color:X

class Figs_Triangle
{
  [key] unBZ Label;
     unBZ Area;
};

[Assodalor] class Figs_CircleToTriangle
{
  Figs_Circle REF ACircle;
  Figs_Triangle REF ATriangle;
};

[Assodalor] class Figs_Covers
  Figs_Triangle REF Over
  Figs_Triangle REF Under
};
```

```
Instance of Figs_Triangle {Label=2;Color="Blue"
Instance of Figs_Triangle {Lable=1;Color="Blue"
Instance of Figs_Circle {Name=1;Color="Blue"};
Instance of Figs_Circle {Name=3;Color="Blue"};
Instance of Figs_Circle {Name=5;color="Blue"};

Instance of Figs_CircleToTriangle
{ ACircle = "Circle.Name=1";
  ATriangle = "Triangle.Label=2";};

Instance of Figs_CircleToTriangle
{ ACircle = "Circle.Name=5";
  ATriangle = "Triangle.Label=2";};

Instance of Figs_CircleToTriangle
{ ACircle = "Circle.Name=5";
  ATriangle = "Triangle.lable=1";};

Instance of Figs_Covers
{ Over = "Triangle.Label=2";
  Under = "Triangle.Label=1";};
```

FIGURE 4.11 Exporting to MOF

The import operation involves storing the information in a local or native format of Mgmt_ABC so its native operations can be used to manipulate the instances. The transformation to a native format is shown in the figure by wrapping the five instances in hexagons. The transformation process must maintain the original keys.

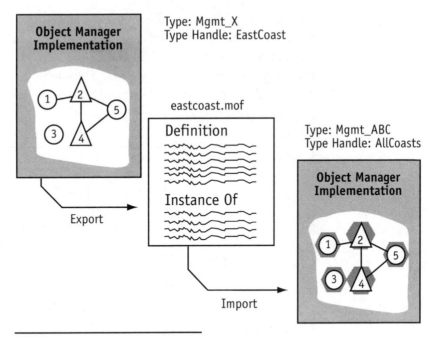

FIGURE 4.12   Information exchange

Weak Associations

CIM provides a mechanism to name instances within the context of other object instances. For instance, if a management tool is handling a local system, then it can refer to the C drive or the D drive. However, if a management tool is handling multiple machines, it must refer to the C drive on machine X and the C drive on machine Y. In other words, the name of the drive must include the name of the hosting machine. CIM supports the notion of weak associations to specify this type of key propagation.

A weak association is defined using a qualifier. For example:

```
Qualifier Weak: boolean = false, Scope(reference),
          Flavor(DisableOverride);
```

The key(s) of the referenced class includes the key(s) of the other participants in the Weak association. This situation occurs when the referenced class identity depends on the identity of other participants in the association.

Figure 4.13 shows an example. There are three classes: Computer-System, Operating System, and Local User. The Operating System class is weak with respect to the Computer System class, since the Runs association is marked weak. Similarly, the Local User class is weak with respect to the Operating System class, since the association is marked weak.

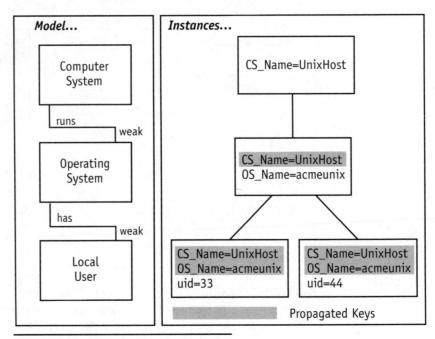

FIGURE 4.13   Example of weak association

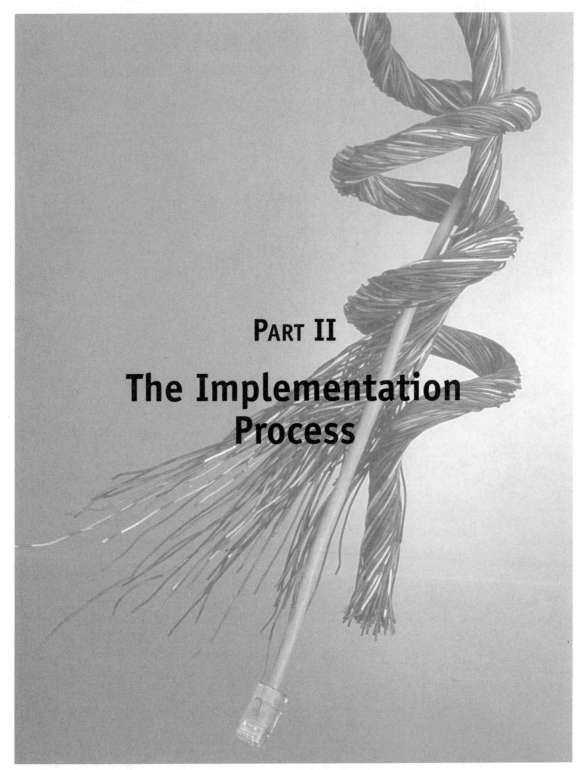

CHAPTER 5

An Overview
of Important
Specifications

As remote access services increases, enterprise directories have been growing more and more in functionality, from simply validation of users to beyond network operating systems (NOS) management. A typical example of increased features is Novell's BorderManager, whose network directory systems (NDS) hold configuration and management information for virtual private network (VPN) tunnels.

Netscape is another example. The company's SuiteSpot 5.0 Mission Control management also provides directory-enabled administration of Netscape client, servers, and application software. Its user profiles are not even stored in the client, but in the server, enabling a client to roam anywhere inside the organization, across town, out of state, or even overseas.

Directory-enabled networks also facilitate the remote authentication dial-in user service (RADIUS) and the dynamic host configuration protocol integration with the domain name system (DNS). Nortel Networks, for instance, has a proprietary service that uses native directory in Microsoft's Windows NT, Novell's NetWare, and UNIX to authenticate RADIUS users.

Lucent Technologies is beginning to offer a fully functional, lower-capacity version of its Internet Directory Server (IDS), which enables Internet, intranet, and on-line service providers to offer directory-based services. Such examples show the importance of DEN and its niche in the ISP market, for service providers anxious to begin deploying directory-enabled services in a cost-effective way without sacrificing functionality.

LDAP version 3, as a specification, is playing a major role in this process. This is the Internet standard that makes directories open and compatible between systems. As discussed in Chapter 2, LDAP is at the core of DEN's base schema. Similarly, Lucent's IDS stores data such as e-mail addresses and subscriber preferences, enabling service providers to offer directory-enabled services including Internet telephony, electronic yellow or white pages, personalized navigation services, and public-key security.

Lucent's IDS is ideal for Internet telephony applications because its dynamic update feature supports up to 200 dynamic updates per second on a two-processor server. Also included in the light version are online backup, fault detection, and built-in recovery systems that support the Internet Directory Server's production-grade services capability.

Lucent's IDS is the most cost-effective LDAP server on the market that supports production-grade services and is scalable. Lucent is also supporting the DEN initiative and its offerings are a major example of the importance of specifications such as LDAP for the full implementation of DEN.

This chapter discusses such specifications, including IPSec and DHCP, and how they affect DEN's specification and implementation. The majority of vendors already agree on the usefulness of and have announced their plans for, DEN.

The Light Directory Access Protocol (LDAP)

Only a few vendors already deploy directory-based implementations, but all of them have in common the adoption of the LDAP for accessing and updating the directories. LDAP's latest version, 3.0, enables client systems, such as hubs, switches, and routers, to read and write directory information.

Although any network equipment manufacturer running LDAP 3.0 will be able to work with a LDAP 3-compliant directory, watch for proprietary implementations, which are more likely to have tighter integration and performance.

Novell's NDS 5.0 supports LDAP 3.0, but use their proprietary Novell client service if performance and response time are important. These two features are critical for DEN's success, so equipment vendors might want to support the Novell interface.

Understanding LDAP

The integration of communications and computing technologies in the 1970s led to the development of new communication technologies. Many of the proprietary systems developed were incompatible with other systems and a standard was necessary to enable equipment and systems from different vendors to interoperate. The Open System Interconnect (OSI) and the Internet were the two major independent standards developed.

The OSI protocols developed slowly, and because running the full protocol stack is resource intensive, they have not been widely deployed, especially in the desktop and small-computer market. In the meantime, TCP/IP and the Internet were developing rapidly and being put into use. Some network vendors also developed proprietary network protocols and products.

An Overview of the X.500

Despite the fact the OSI protocols where not gaining much momentum, they addressed important issues for large systems being developed for the Internet. An example is directory services. The Comite Commultatif Internationale de Telegraphique et Telephonique (CCITT) created the X.500 standard in 1988; this then became ISO 9594, Data Communications Network Directory, Recommendations X.500-X.521. We know it as X.500.

A main distinction of X.500 is that it organizes directory entries in a hierarchical name space capable of supporting large amounts of information. It also defines powerful search capabilities to make retrieving information easier. Because of its functionality and scalability, X.500 is often used with add-on modules for interoperation between incompatible directory services.

X.500 specifies that communication between the directory client and the directory server uses the directory access protocol (DAP). However, as an application-layer protocol, DAP requires the entire OSI protocol stack to operate. Supporting the OSI protocol stack requires more resources than are available in many small environments. Therefore, an interface to an X.500 directory server using a less resource-intensive or lightweight protocol was desirable.

Figure 5.1 shows a layout of how X.500 uses address and details templates to gain access to the DEN schema. Consider this schema the cornerstone of X.500 functionality and features.

The concept of directory is the core of X.500, an information system that records data about a set of *objects of interest*. Designed to be used as the basis of a single global directory for all objects of interest, X.500 is typically used on implementations to record information about people, processes, devices, and so on that revolves around communication in an organization. Microsoft Exchange Server provides an implementation of an X.500 directory.

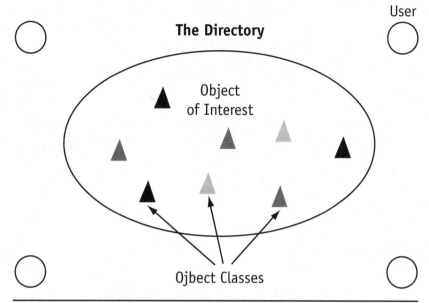

FIGURE 5.1 A layout of how X.500 address and details templates gain access to the DEN schema

NOTE

An *object of interest* is an object which may be subject to an information request by a *user*, either a human or computer process requesting information from the directory.

The information about the objects in the directory is collectively stored in the *directory information base* (DIB). The DIB acts as an interface between the directory users and the processes providing directory services. Objects in the directory correspond to entries in the DIB. The DIB can be organized in whatever manner suits the user, subject to consistency rules. Each type of object, known as an *object class*, is recognized by the directory which will only allow the creation of those objects with defined object classes. When created and modified, the object must be consistent with the rules of its object class. Figure 5.2 provides a layout of the directory information tree.

To give organization and a naming structure to what could be an arbitrarily large number of entries in the DIB, a hierarchy is implemented. This hierarchy of structure and DIB entries is called the *Directory Information Tree* (DIT). The DIT is the combination of a root entry representing the starting point of the tree, leaf entries representing actual objects (leaf objects) and non-leaf entries representing the structure of the DIT. Non-leaf entries are also called *container entries* (corresponding to container objects). The main difference between container entries and leaf entries is that container entries can contain other container and leaf entries. Leaf entries do not contain other entries and usually represent an actual object of interest. If objects are created under a leaf object, that leaf object becomes a container object.

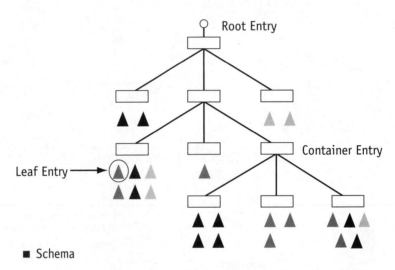

FIGURE 5.2   The Directory Information Tree

In the DIB, entries must be named unambiguously to identify them within its scope and must be named uniquely within the entire DIB. A name is a data value assigned to the DIB entry which identifies the object of interest, as shown in Figure 5.3.

To identify the object within the entire DIB, a unique name must be constructed identifying through organization units (Oun) not only the unambiguous name but also the location within the DIB.

Since the DIB has a hierarchical structure via the DIT, the unique name for the object can be constructed from the DIT structure. This unique name, a combination of the DIT structure and the object's unambiguous name, is known as the *distinguished name* (DN). All entries (and therefore all objects) in the DIT have unique distinguished names. The distinguished name is an ordered list of a series of *relative distinguished names* (RDNs) which serve to identify the leaf and container entries corresponding to the exact location of the entry in the DIT relative to the root entry.

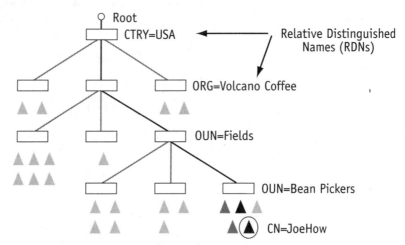

■ Distinguished name for JoeHow object:

[CTRY=USA, ORG=Volcano Coffee, OUN=Fields, OUN=Bean Pickers, CN=JoeHow]

FIGURE 5.3   Naming conventions

Once the directory is created and organized with a hierarchical structure, directory schema, and a naming scheme, its information must be available to users, as depicted in Figure 5.4. A *directory user agent* (DUA) is used to abstract the directory for the users. The DUA is the mechanism by which directory users gain access to and maintain the directory itself.

A component called a *directory service agent* (DSA) is at the entry point of the directory used by the DUA, which is responsible for transparently handling DUA requests either itself or consulting with other DSAs within the directory. The set of DUAs and DSAs managed by a single organization is called a *directory management domain* (DMD).

The directory may be one large pool of information as abstracted by the DSA, as shown in Figure 5.5. However, each DSA does not have to store the entire pool of information. The directory can be distributed among the DSAs. Each DSA can hold a subset of the

DIT, called its *fragment*, and each DSA knows which parts of the DIT are stored on which DSA.

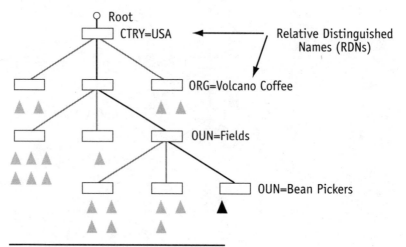

FIGURE 5.4   Directory services to the user

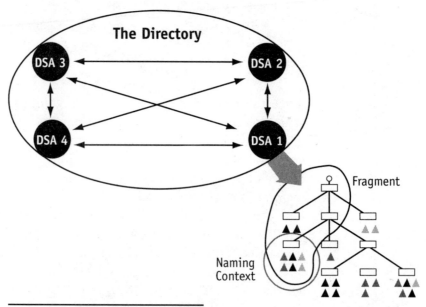

FIGURE 5.5   Distributing the directory

When a DUA requests access for a DIT entry not stored on the DSA, the DSA can employ *chaining* or *referral* to service the original DUA request. While chaining and referral work to service the original request, they will have an impact on the time it takes the DUA to access the directory.

If access time is a problem, an alternative is to store the entire directory at each DSA, which will copy its fragment and ongoing changes to its fragment to all the other DSAs through a process called *replication*. Replication ensures that each DSA has a reasonably recent copy of the directory. The unit of distribution when replicating a fragment is a branch or sub-tree of the DIT known as a *naming context*. The main difference between a fragment and a naming context is that a fragment is not confined to a branch of the DIT, but can be multiplied as branches in various parts of the DIT.

Using LDAP as a Lightweight Access to X.500

LDAP was developed as a lightweight alternative to DAP, requiring the lighter weight and more popular TCP/IP protocol stack rather than the OSI protocol stack. LDAP also simplifies some X.500 operations, even though it does omit some of X.500's features.

The first version of LDAP was defined in X.500 Lightweight Access Protocol (RFC 1487), which was replaced by Lightweight Directory Access Protocol (RFC 1777). LDAP further refines the ideas and protocols of Direct Access Storage (DAS) and DIXIE. It is more implementation neutral and reduces the complexity of clients to encourage the deployment of directory-enabled applications. Much of the work on DIXIE and LDAP was carried out at the University of Michigan, which provides reference implementations of LDAP and maintains LDAP-related Web pages and mailing lists. LDAP version 3 is defined by Lightweight Directory Access Protocol (v3) (RFC 2251).

LDAP defines a communication protocol. That is, it defines the transport and format of messages used by a client to access data in an X.500-like directory. Despite its tight relationship with DEN, LDAP does not define the directory service itself, even though LDAP is often seen as one.

To better understand LDAP consider this scenario: an application client program initiates an LDAP message by calling an LDAP API. But an X.500 directory server does not understand LDAP messages. The LDAP client and X.500 server even use different communication protocols (TCP/IP vs. OSI). In fact, the LDAP client communicates with a gateway process that forwards requests to the X.500 directory server, as shown in Figure 5.6. This gateway is known as an *LDAP server*. It services requests from the LDAP client by becoming a client of the X.500 server. The LDAP server must communicate using both TCP/IP and OSI.

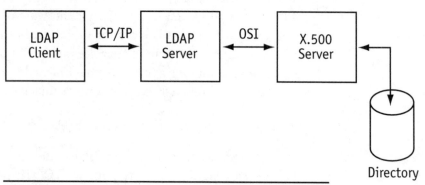

FIGURE 5.6   LDAP server acting as a gateway to an X.500 server

As LDAP's use proliferated and its benefits became apparent, people who did not have X.500 servers or the environments to support them wanted to build directories that could be accessed by LDAP clients. They wanted to have the LDAP server store and access the directory itself instead of only acting as a gateway to X.500 servers, as shown in Figure 5.7. A standalone LDAP server eliminates the need for the OSI protocol stack. This makes the LDAP server much more complicated, since it must store and retrieve directory entries.

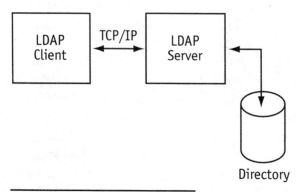

FIGURE 5.7   Standalone LDAP server

Application developers can also take advantage of LDAP to develop next-generation directory-enabled applications (here is where DEN comes in). A common directory infrastructure encourages new uses. DEN's proposal is to allow information about network configuration, protocol information, router characteristics, and so on to be stored in an LDAP directory. The availability of this information in a common format will allow the intelligent management and provisioning of network resources. These examples show the diverse uses of directory-enabled applications supported by a common directory infrastructure accessed with LDAP.

Most of the latest Web browsers, such as Netscape's Communicator or Microsoft's Internet Explorer are LDAP-enabled. They can look up entries in an LDAP directory. In Figure 5.8, I used Netscape Communicator as an example. During the installation of Netscape Communicator, a series of public LDAP services are already configured as selectable directories for searching. These directories are available by selecting the Search Directory from the Edit pulldown menu in the Navigator window, as shown in Figure 5.8

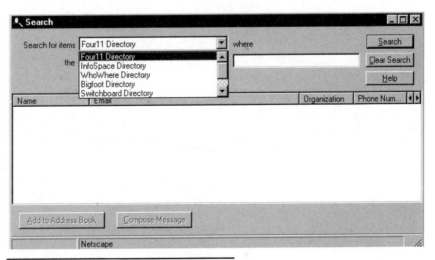

FIGURE 5.8 Searching an Internet directory

The Yahoo site also uses LDAP. Figure 5.9 shows searching criteria to find all listed e-mail addresses of the employees at ARC. Once all fields are selected or filled as required, a click on the Search button sends the request to the selected service and returns the results in a short while. Figure 5.10 shows the search results for people associated with the ARC. Note that only the first 100 records are returned, which is a configurable option in a browser.

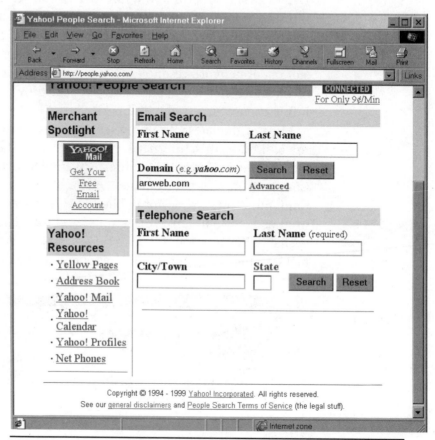

FIGURE 5.9   Searching Yahoo for people associated with the organization ARC

Understanding LDAP's Four Base Models

LDAP can be better understood if we consider its four base models:

✦ **Information:** The structure of information stored in an LDAP directory

✦ **Naming:** How information in an LDAP directory is organized and identified

✦ **Function:** What operations can be performed on the information stored in an LDAP directory

✦ **Security:** How the information in an LDAP directory can be protected from unauthorized access.

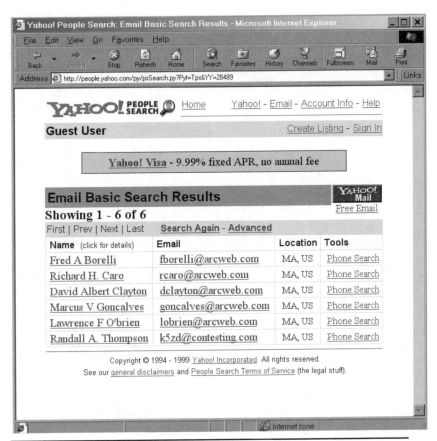

FIGURE 5.10 Results of the query, showing the names and e-mail addresses as stored in the directory

The Information Model

The basic unit of information stored in the directory is called an *entry*. Entries represent objects of interest in the real world such as people, servers, organizations, and so on. Entries are composed of a collection of attributes that contain information about the object. Each attribute has a type and one or more values. The type of attribute is associated with syntax. The syntax specifies what kind of values can be stored.

Therefore, it is possible that the directory entry for an organization would contain multiple values in this attribute—that is an organization or person represented by the entity would have multiple fax numbers, for example. The relationship between a directory entry and its attributes and their values is shown in Figure 5.11

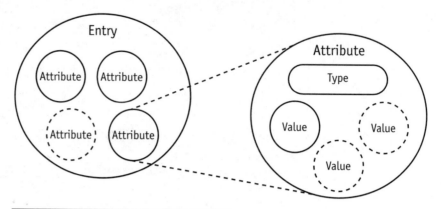

FIGURE 5.11   Entry, attributes, and values

In addition to defining what data can be stored as the value of an attribute, attribute syntax also defines how those values behave during searches and other directory operations. The attribute telephoneNumber, for example, has a syntax that specifies:

✦ Lexicographic ordering
✦ Case, spaces, and dashes that are ignored during the comparisons
✦ Values that must be character strings.

For instance, using the correct definitions, the telephone numbers "781-358-4785", "781358-4785," and "7813584785" have the same value. A few of the syntaxes defined for LDAP are listed in Figure 5.12.

Figure 5.13 lists some common attributes. Some attributes have alias names that can be used wherever the full attribute name is used. For example, cn can be used when referring to the attribute commonName.

The Naming Model

The LDAP naming model defines how entries are identified and organized. Entries are organized in a tree-like structure called the DIT, similar to X.500. Entries are arranged within the DIT based on their DN, a unique name that unambiguously identifies a single entry. DNs are made up of a sequence of RDNs. Each RDN in a DN corresponds to a branch in the DIT leading from the root of the DIT to the directory entry.

Syntax	Description
bin	Binary information.
ces	Case exact string, also known as a "directory string", case is significant during comparisons.
cis	Case ignore string. Case is not significant during comparisons.
tel	Telephone number. The numbers are treated as text, but all blanks and dashes are ignored.
dn	Distinguished name.
Generalized Time	Year, month, day, and time represented as a printable string.
Postal Address	Postal address with line separated by "$" characters.

FIGURE 5.12   List of some syntaxes defined for LDAP

Attribute, Alias	Syntax	Description	Example
commonName, cn	cis	Common name of an entry	John Smith
surname, sn	cis	Surname (last name) of a person	Smith
telephoneNumber	tel	Telephone number	512-838-6008
organizationalUnitName, ou	cis	Name or an organizational unity	itso
owner	dn	Distinguished name of the person that owns the entry	cn=John Smith, o=IBM, c=US
organization, o	cis	Name of an organziation	IBM
jpegPhoto	bin	Photographic image in JPEG format	Photograph of John Smith

FIGURE 5.13   Common LDAP attributes

Each RDN is derived from the attributes of the directory entry. In a simple and common case, an RDN has the form < attribute name >

= < value >. A DN is composed of a sequence of RDNs separated by commas.

An example of a DIT is shown in Figure 5.14. The example is simple, but can be used to illustrate some basic concepts. Each box represents a directory entry. The root directory entry is conceptual, but does not actually exist. Attributes are listed inside each entry. The list of attributes shown is not complete. For example, the entry for the country DE (c=DE) could have an attribute called description with the value Germany.

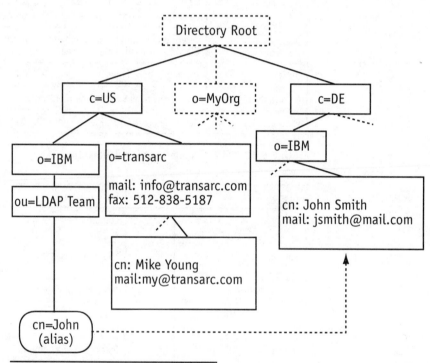

FIGURE 5.14   Directory Information Tree

The organization of the entries in the DIT is restricted by their corresponding object class definitions. It is usual to follow either a geographical or an organizational scheme.

The Functional Model

LDAP defines operations for accessing and modifying directory entries. LDAP operations can be divided into the following three categories:

✦ **Query:** Which includes the search and compare operations used to retrieve information from a directory

✦ **Update:** Which includes the add, delete, modify, and modify RDN operations used to update stored information in a directory

✦ **Authentication:** Which includes the bind, unbind, and abandon operations used to connect and disconnect to and from an LDAP server, establish access rights and protect information.

The most common operation is search. The search operation is very flexible and has some of the most complex options. It allows a client to request that an LDAP server search through some portion of the DIT for information meeting user-specified criteria, then read and list the result(s). The search can be general or specific. The search operation makes it possible to specify the starting point within the DIT, how deep within the DIT to search, what attributes an entry must have to be considered a match, and what attributes to return for matched entries.

To perform a search, the following parameters must be specified, as described in Figure 5.15:

✦ **Base:** A DN that defines the starting point, called the *base object*, of the search. The base object is a node within the DIT.

✦ **Scope:** This specifies how deep within the DIT to search from the base object. There are three choices: baseObject, singleLevel, and wholeSubtree. If baseObject is specified, only the base object is examined. If singleLevel is specified, only the immediate children of the base object are examined; the base object itself is not examined. If wholeSubtree is specified, the base object and all of its descendants are examined.

✦ **Search Filter:** This specifies the criteria an entry must match to be returned from a search. The search filter is a Boolean combination of attribute value assertions. An attribute value assertion tests the value of an attribute for equality, less than or equal, and so on.

✦ **Attributes to Return:** This specifies that attributes to be retrieved from entries must match the search criteria. Since an entry may have many attributes, this allows users to see only the attributes they are interested in. Normally, a user is interested in the value of the attributes.

✦ **Alias Dereferencing:** This specifies if aliases are dereferenced—that is, if the alias entry itself or the entry it points to is used. Aliases can be dereferenced or not when locating the base object and/or when searching under the base object. If aliases are dereferenced, then they are alternate names for objects of interest in the directory. Not dereferencing aliases allows the alias entries themselves to be examined.

✦ **Limits:** Searches can be general, examining large subtrees and causing many entries to be returned. The user can specify time and size limits to prevent wayward searching from consuming too many resources. The size limit restricts the number of entries returned from the search. The time limit limits the total time of the search. Servers are free to impose stricter limits than requested by the client.

The Security Model

The security model is based on the bind operation and several different bind operations are possible. One possibility is when a client requesting access supplies a DN identifying itself along with a simple clear-text password. If no DN and password is declared, the LDAP server assumes an anonymous session. The use of clear text passwords is discouraged when the underlying transport service cannot guarantee confidentiality and may therefore result in disclosure of the password to unauthorized parties.

A Kerberos bind is possible in LDAP Version 2, but this has become discouraged in LDAP Version 3. Instead, LDAP v3 provides a bind command supporting the Simple Authentication and Security Layer (SASL) mechanism. This is a general authentication framework where several different authentication methods are available for authenticating the client to the server; one of them is Kerberos.

Vendors like Netscape and IBM have already extended the LDAP protocol and added some SSL-specific commands so that an encrypted TCP/IP connection is possible, thus providing a means for eliminating the need to send a DN and a password unprotected over the network.

Once a client is identified, access control information can be consulted to determine whether or not the client has sufficient access permissions to do what it is requesting.

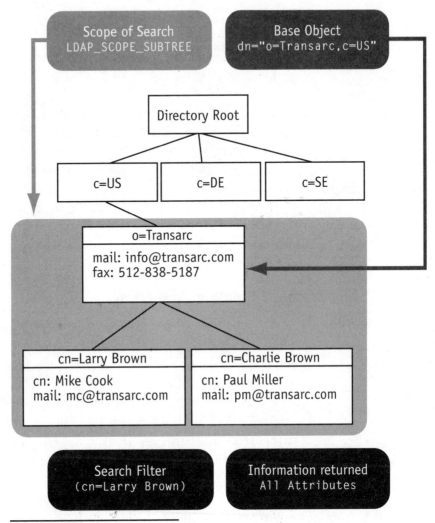

FIGURE 5.15 Search parameters

Authenticating PPP

This section was based on the Internet draft entitled "Lightweight Directory Access Protocol (v3): Extension for PPP Authentication," by Bernard Aboba of Microsoft.

For a full version of this document, look for the file <draft-aboba-ppp-01.txt> at the Internet-Drafts Shadow Directories on **ds.internic.net** (U.S. East Coast), **nic.nordu.net** (Europe), **ftp.isi.edu** (U.S. West Coast), or **munnari.oz.au** (Pacific Rim).

NOTE

The PPP authentication operation for LDAP provides for PPP authentication in an LDAP association and is defined in terms of an LDAP extended operation. This extended operation should be very useful in integrating authentication protocols such as RADIUS and TACACS + with LDAP-based directory services.

Currently RADIUS and TACACS + authentication servers typically include their own stores of user data. In order to simplify user administration, these services should be integrated with an LDAP-based directory service.

Integrating PPP Authentication Methods

In order for a RADIUS server to respond, an Access-Request's credentials must be validated. However, current LDAP security mechanisms do not support PPP authentication methods so that extensions or protocol modifications are required.

There are several alternatives available, however. One is to add support for PPP authentication methods to SASL, and utilize the secure BIND mechanisms. In this case, the RADIUS server will impersonate the user and bind using the credentials submitted in the Access-Request. Thus, only the user would need to have the access rights to retrieve RADIUS attributes from the directory. There would be no need to make these attributes accessible to a privileged account used by the RADIUS server, or to any network devices; this would be important from the security point of view.

Using this alternative, support for PPP authentication methods would be added to SASL. The RADIUS server would set up an SSL/TLS connection on startup, and would execute a BIND operation for each authentication; the server would only UNBIND on shutdown. Merely adding Challenge Handshake Authentication Protocol (CHAP) support to SASL will not be a solution since an LDAP-server using a CHAP extension to SASL would generate its own challenge, rather than accepting a CHAP challenge and response submitted to it by the RADIUS server.

To solve the problem, it must be possible to submit both the CHAP challenge and the response to SASL. However, making it possible to authenticate to an LDAP server using such a mechanism is not desirable since it would make LDAP authentication susceptible to a replay attack.

Another alternative is to provide support for PPP authentication within an LDAP extended operation. In this alternative, the RADIUS server binds to the directory on startup using a special account, and unbinds on shutdown. In between the bind and unbind, the RADIUS server may submit as many PPP authentication requests as necessary. In this scenario, the account used by the RADIUS server needs to have the access rights to retrieve RADIUS attributes for any user.

Understanding PPP Authentication

PPP authentication is an extended operation initiated by an LDAP client (RADIUS server) in order to request authentication of a user by the LDAP-based directory. The LDAP client sends a PPP authentication request to the LDAP server, indicating the PPP authentication method, and including the user's credentials; the server then responds with a message indicating the success or failure of the authentication.

When the RADIUS server receives an Access-Request packet from a Network Attached Storeage (NAS) or VPN server, it examines the User-Name attribute to determine the user that is being authenticated. Based on the User-Name, the server may also retrieve the authentication Type attribute for the user, and will then check the authentication method specified in the Access-Request against the permitted types. If there is a mismatch, then the server will formulate and send an Access-Reject packet.

If the user authentication is unsuccessful, then the RADIUS server will formulate and send an Access-Reject packet. If the user is successfully authenticated then the RADIUS server will formulate an Access-Accept based on the attributes retrieved from the LDAP-based directory service.

Security Considerations

Enabling an LDAP-based directory service to perform PPP authentication operations in an efficient manner may result in a number of security threats, including password guessing attacks and sniffing attacks. In order to prevent a rogue RADIUS server from initiating password-guessing attacks, implementations should close a connection after a number of consecutive authentication failures.

In order to prevent sniffing of passwords, where Password Authentication Protocol (PAP) authentication is being used for transmission of cleartext passwords, the RADIUS server must ensure confidentiality by using SSL/TLS or IPSEC. An LDAP server receiving a PAP authentication request representing a cleartext password without confidentiality services in place should return an error message.

Dynamic Attributes and Schema for RADIUS

This section defines the dynamic attributes used by the Remote Access Dialin User Service (RADIUS). These attributes are written to a dynamic directory service by the RADIUS server in order to provide information about sessions in progress. This information can be used to provide for control of simultaneous logins, or for detection or tracking of security incidents in progress.

The RADIUS protocol supports authentication, authorization, and accounting for dialup users. To date, RADIUS servers have retrieved their configuration from user databases and/or flat configuration files. In order to consolidate stores of user information, it is desirable to integrate a RADIUS with an LDAP-based directory service.

A dynamic directory service can be used to store these and other attributes relating to sessions in progress. Such information can be useful for a variety of purposes including security incident response, simultaneous usage control, or monitoring of connection quality, login time, and packet size or bandwidth usage..

A RADIUS server should typically create an entry in the dynamic directory service after a successful authentication, and will delete the entry when the user logs off. However, some implementations may find it desirable to allow persistence of entries relating to failed authentication or logged-off users. In this case, a refresh interval is typically set so that the entries will time out after an appropriate interval.

Supporting DHCP

This section is based on T. Miller, A. Patel and P. Rao, informational draft entitled "Lightweight Directory Access Protocol (v3): Schema for Dynamic Host Configuration Protocol (DHCP)" (< draft-miller-dhcp-ldap-schema-00.txt >).

Ideally, DHCP servers should be integrated with an LDAP-based directory service, allowing an organization to maintain a single store of IP addresses and other configuration data provided to clients using the DHCP protocol. Integration of DHCP into LDAP directories can reduce administrative overhead and eliminates the need to maintain multiple server-centric configuration databases.

The schema can be useful for providing a standardized format for the representation of attributes needed by DHCP implementations within LDAP-based directory services.

Overview

DHCP is a protocol which allows IP addresses to be assigned to devices from a server, usually at boot time. DHCP servers typically allow an administrator to assign an address to a device dynamically from a pool of addresses; if necessary, a specific address can be assigned to a device based upon an identifier such as a MAC address.

In addition to assigning IP addresses to clients, DHCP can be used to provide other configuration information to devices, such as the IP address of DNS servers, the address of a default router, or many other configuration parameters.

Organizations need to manage addresses and device configuration for widely dispersed networks. While many DHCP servers may be needed within an organization's network, management of addresses and configuration from a single point could substantially enhance network management tasks. Integrating DHCP into an LDAP directory allows for a single point of administration for a distributed set of DHCP servers.

DNS/DHCP Locator

The DNS/DHCP Locator object is an object used to store global information relevant for both DNS and DHCP.

These two services interact in some cases, such as for dynamic DNS updates. The administration of the two services is often linked.

The Locator object has two purposes. First, it contains DNs of other objects of interest for DNS and DHCP. For DHCP these include subnets, subnet pools, and DHCP servers. By having DNs of all these objects, an application such as a GUI is able to present a list of all these objects without needing to search the entire tree for the objects. Instead, the application just needs to find the locator, then read the DNs of the other objects. This can offer a significant performance advantage.

The second DHCP use of the locator object is to store configuration information that is to apply to the entire tree. This global configuration, as for DHCP option values, is to apply to the entire tree unless it is overridden at a lower level of the tree. In the case of DHCP options, the global values in the locator object could be overridden at the Subnet object or IP address object levels.

Subnet

The Subnet object represents an IP subnet. As would be expected, it has an address and mask to define the subnet. The Subnet object is designed to be placed in the part of the tree representing the location it is serving; it is contained by an O, OU, C, or L (Organization, Organizational Unit, Locality, or Country).

The Subnet object also has attributes for configuration that apply to the entire subnet. For example, there is an attribute to specify the lease time for addresses assigned dynamically from the subnet. An important attribute in the subnet is DHCPConfigOptions, which indicates the values to be passed to the client when it requests DHCP options. DHCP options not specified at the subnet level can be inherited from the DNS/DHCP Locator object. This allows an administrator to configure options for an entire enterprise once, and then specify exceptions at the subnet level.

Subnet Address Range

The Subnet Address Range object identifies a range of addresses within a subnet. It is a leaf object that is contained under the subnet and has a type attribute to identify it as one of several types of ranges available for dynamic address assignment or as a set of addresses that an administrator wishes to exclude from address assignment.

IP Address

The IP Address object represents a single IP address. It is a leaf object that is contained under a subnet. An administrator creates the IP Address object when a specific address needs to be assigned to a device. The IP Address object has as attributes a MAC address and client ID. When a request is received from a client for an address the MAC address or client ID is compared to these attributes to determine what address to provide the client.

The IP Address object has attributes similar to those of the Subnet object which apply to the specific address instead of the entire subnet. One attribute is DHCP options. When a client requests DHCP options they first come from the IP address object if an individual option is specified. For those options not specified at the IP Address object level, the DHCP server will first check the Subnet object and then the DNS/DHCP Locator object.

In addition to being created by administrators, IP Address objects can be created by a DHCP server to represent IP address assignments in the directory. The IP Address object has attributes to identify when the lease will expire and when it was last renewed.

The IP Address object has a type attribute to indicate whether it was created to represent a static or dynamic address assignment. This attribute can also indicate that the IP Address object represents an address currently not assigned. This allows a DHCP server to mark an attribute, rather than delete an object, when an address lease expires.

Subnet Pool

The Subnet Pool object is used to group together a set of subnets. It is a leaf object that is contained in any O, OU, L, or C. The subnet pool has a multi-valued attribute with distinguished names of Subnet objects.

The primary purpose of the Subnet Pool object is to group together subnets when a DHCP relay agent is forwarding multiple subnets to a DHCP server. Since only the address of the DHCP relay agent is received by the DHCP server, it is impossible for it to assign addresses from multiple subnets, without having a way to group them together.

DHCP Server

The DHCP Server object has attributes for server-oriented configuration, including DNs of subnet address ranges assigned to the server for dynamic address assignment.

Attributes have also been defined to provide for a fail-over capability. The DHCP server object has attributes with syntax of DN to identify a primary and a secondary DHCP server that will provide the DHCP service represented by this object.

CHAPTER **6**

Policy-Powered Networks

During Summer 1998 3Com Australia and New Zealand announced the industry's first practical plan for deploying policy-powered networks (PPNs). The PPNs provided for advanced intelligence to enable enterprises more easily and comprehensively to enforce business policies on information access security, information delivery, such as class and quality of service (QoS), network equipment monitoring and equipment configuration.

Based on 3Com networking solutions and open standards for interoperability with other networking vendors' products, PPNs have the intelligence to enforce these policies dynamically, according to user, workgroups, departments, date, time of day, and even the level of network congestion.

3Com policy-powered networks are easier to configure than conventionally managed networks; this can dramatically reduce current network administrative costs, and offer the control required for next-generation converged voice/video/data networks, virtual private networks, and extranets for electronic commerce.

The PPN plan includes a five-step guideline that covers networking hardware deployment, types of software standards, directory support and network monitoring procedures, as well as the industry's most comprehensive policy framework based on industry standards for incorporating 3Com's and other vendors' equipment.

PPN enables IT groups to improve their current data networks and cost-effectively lay the foundation for the converged voice/video/data, electronic commerce, and virtual private networks that will soon be commonplace.

Users can deploy PPNs using a five-step process, which includes:

✦ Baselining their network using analysis tools
✦ Installing "smart bandwidth devices" (networking equipment with advanced policy intelligence)
✦ Developing company policies and implementation plans for security, class of service/quality of service, monitoring, and configuration
✦ Setting policies using the Policy Manager applications
✦ Monitoring the effectiveness of policies and appropriately tuning the network.

Nonetheless, policy-powered networks are much more complex than device configuration management since the directories are just databases. The issue here is that directories are not designed to collect information from a variety of devices and other sources scattered throughout a network, and develop a policy decision based thereon.

This chapter discusses policy-powered networks, the benefits they offer and the challenges they face.

The Role of Policy-Powered Networks[1]

A PPN must address a real problem that needs to be solved, such as traffic prioritization and security as well as additional capabilities dictated by the industry.

There are four main roles required in a policy-powered network, as shown in Figure 6.1:

✦ **Information storage:** Information storage is concerned with the back-end data stores, the replication of data throughout the network, and the schema of the directory information.

✦ **Policy requester:** A policy request is triggered when a policy client observes a demand to access network resources. The trigger could be many things, such as the launch of an application, for example or a dial-in to a remote accesses server port. However, the policy request does not necessarily require the deployment of custom software.

✦ **Policy interpreter:** Policy interpretation is the role performed by the network device that manages state and evaluates the particulars of the resource request.

✦ **Policy enforcer:** Enforcement is the role performed by a network to ensure that the policy leases are realized. The decision made by the enforcement policy is carried out by the specific hardware/software features residing in the policy client, such as packet filtering, bandwidth reservation, etc.

---

1 This section was based on 3Com's white paper "3Com Strategy for Delivering Policy-Powered Networking," found at the company's URL **http://www.3com.com/ technology/tech_net/white_papers/500670.html#networking**. Check that site for additional information.

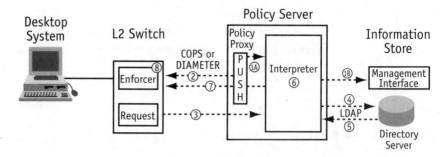

FIGURE 6.1   Basic model for policy-powered networking

3Com offers an example to demonstrate how PPN works:

> Usually, IT groups use the policy manager application to restrict user access to employee records in the HR database according to permissions contained in the user's profile and the time-of-day/date, in addition to the traditional application password. At 11:00 a.m. on Friday, user John Smith attempts to make a query of the HR database.
>
> The launch of the application to access the HR database triggers a policy request. The policy enforcer (the Layer 3 switch) submits the request to the policy server, asking it to make a policy decision. The policy server performs a policy interpretation role, managing state and evaluating the particulars of each resource request. The interpreter may consult a variety of different information sources before it can arrive at a policy decision.

In the above example, two information stores must be accessed in order to decide if access should be granted or denied: the LDAP-enabled directory and the Network Time Protocol (NTP) server. The policy server uses LDAP to access John Smith's user profile from the directory server and NTP to access the time server. Then the policy server formulates a response to send to the policy client or enforcer in the form of a policy lease. The policy lease instructs the policy client whether it should permit or deny John Smith's request to access the HR database.

A network device performs the enforcement role. The specific hardware/software features residing in the policy-enabled network device (such as packet filtering, bandwidth reservation, traffic prioritization, multiple forwarding queues, etc.) carry out enforcement of policy decisions. 3Com has recently launched a new generation of networking devices that have the specific hardware and software features required to enforce policy decisions (for example, multiple queues in switches to support traffic prioritization). In our example, the Layer 3 switch functions as the enforcement device, ensuring policy compliance by either blocking or forwarding John Smith's HR database query.

Benefits of Policy-Powered Networking

Significant benefits can be gained by organizations that take the time to deploy a network capable of supporting policy-powered networking:

✦ **Centralized end-to-end policy management:** This ensures that business objectives are being met in a reliable and predictable manner
✦ **Scalability:** The larger the network, the greater the benefit of policy-powered networking
✦ **Consistency:** With single directory service users, obtain the same configuration, regardless of whether they connect to the network locally or remotely.

Delivering Policy-Powered Networks

According to 3Com, vendors seeking to provide policy-powered networking solutions will be required to offer much more than simple support for policy transactions between policy clients and a policy server. They will need to offer solutions that:

✦ Ensure consistent behavior across the entire network
✦ Scale as the network grows
✦ Do not require massive upgrades
✦ Operate in a multivendor environment
✦ Allow the network to function as a unified system to respond to rapidly changing business climates.

Network administrators face their most critical challenges at network interfaces; the LAN/WAN interface is one of the most obvious. Other interfaces include the desktop/workgroup boundary, the workgroup/core boundary, the enterprise/service provider boundary, and the WAN interface between service providers, as shown in Figure 6.2

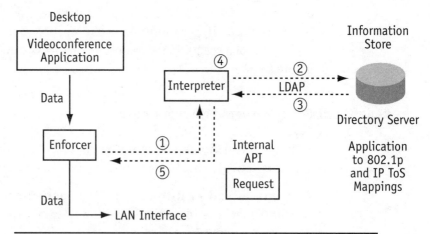

FIGURE 6.2   Policy consistency is required at critical network interfaces

Policies are strategic at these interfaces, as they exercise substantial changes in security, administrative control, performance, and/or cost. Devices on either side of these boundaries must behave according to a common set of policy rules. Here is where policy-powered networks are required to maintain consistent behavior that supports corporate goals.

When establishing policy for their network, network administrators must define enterprise-wide policies at a very high level, without worrying about the specific technical details of policy enforcement across a variety of different network nodes. For instance, as depicted in 3Com's paper listed above, a network administrator might want to implement a general policy rule stating, "Accounting traffic is business-critical while PointCast traffic is less than best effort." The separate, device-specific configurations required to enforce this high-level policy across an enterprise network are depicted in Figure 6.3.

When attempting to implement an enterprise-wide policy, realize that there are different types of network nodes, each with distinct policy enforcement and policy communication capabilities. Some devices actively solicit policy decisions from a policy server, while others do not. Some nodes may speak a policy transaction protocol and others do not. For some applications in a latency-sensitive environment, a single node may be required to function as the requester, enforcer, and interpreter. For other applications, as in enforcing a security policy, the roles may need to be performed separately to ensure a confidential security transaction.

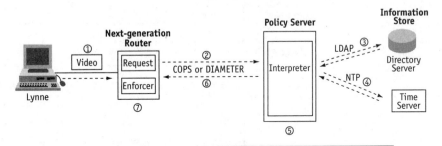

FIGURE 6.3 Different enforcement techniques across an enterprise network

I would like to emphasize that 3Com did a superb job understanding these challenges to the idealized policy transaction model. As a result, the company refined its framework for delivering policy-powered networks. According to their white paper, the goal was to develop a universal model suitable for discussing policy issues within the context of DEN/DMTF and the industry in general. 3Com received a very positive response during its presentation of PPN to the DEN/DMTF in March 1998. This clearly shows the impact of 3Com's framework in providing an environment for developing specific policy applications and determining which elements in the network perform the critical roles of requester, enforcer, and interpreter.

The Four Types of Policy-Enforcement Devices

The PPN framework assumes there are four classes of policy-enforcing network nodes. The model establishes a 2x2 matrix, as shown in Figure 6.4, consisting of active versus passive devices, and policy versus legacy devices. An active device is one that can issue queries to a policy server, while a passive device cannot.

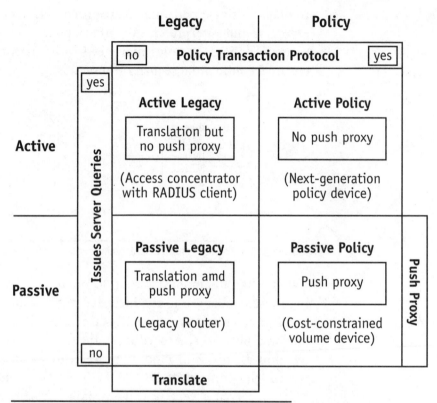

FIGURE 6.4 Four classes of policy-enforcement devices

The following points should be kept in mind when looking at Figure 6.4:

✦ Some devices were deployed before the development of policy standards' such as legacy systems by the IETF. These devices require the policy server to translate the policy decision to each device's legacy protocol.

✦ Other devices, such as passive legacy and passive policy, do not query a policy server either because constant queries would inhibit the forwarding capabilities of the system, or because the devices are too cost-restrained to include a policy client. Thus, the policy server must actively push the policy decision out to these types of devices, since the device lacks the features to do so or is too busy or low-margin to afford the extra cost or cycles of an active policy client.

◆ Only new devices implementing a policy transaction protocol fit cleanly into the basic 3Com model and do not require translation or a push proxy by the policy server.

For a policy-powered network to enhance performance and solve real IT problems, it will need to be pervasive and consistent, being capable of communicating policy decisions to all four types of network nodes, if it is to establish consistent enterprise-wide policies across new and legacy devices. Also, end-to-end policy-powered networks require highly capable network enforcement devices that implement sophisticated packet filtering capabilities, packet scheduling algorithms, and multiple priority queues.

Proxies in Policies

Some network devices do not query a policy server because they are too busy forwarding traffic. Others do not speak a policy transaction protocol, or can be cost-constrained, or even not experience events that would trigger them to request a policy decision. These devices can only be configured to enforce policy via a device-specific method. Policy proxies facilitate the deployment of policy-powered networks by allowing these types of devices to enforce enterprise-wide policies and by providing a migration strategy as the industry waits for policy transaction protocols to mature. In this role, a policy proxy performs four basic functions:

◆ The policy proxy maintains a list of devices for which it is responsible.
◆ Much like a policy server, a policy proxy may be required to translate an existing protocol, such as RADIUS, and convert it to another protocol, such as LDAPv3.
◆ The policy proxy pushes policy to passive devices that cannot query the policy server. This requires that the policy server know which types of devices are capable of performing which type of enforcement, and selectively call on the proper proxy to push the enforcement commands to those devices.
◆ The policy proxy maintains state and monitors the status of the devices for which it is proxying to maintain current policies.

Figure 6.5 shows that for each of the four types of policy-enforcement nodes, a policy transaction may include a translation function, a push function, both functions, or neither function. The specific nature of the enforcement device combined with the kind of policy type dictate which proxy functions are required by the proxy server.

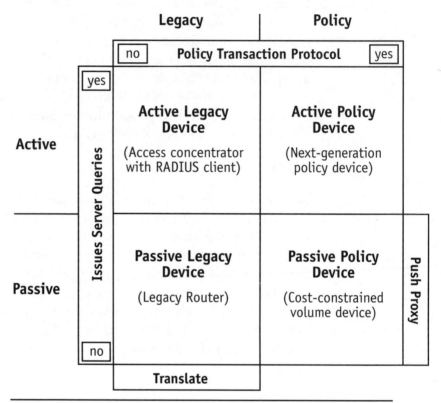

FIGURE 6.5   Policy proxy interaction with the four types of network devices

Policy Transaction Models

This section discusses 3Com's PPN policy transaction models and how the framework can be applied to specific policy transactions.

Active Policy Device: Layer 3 Packet Filtering

An active policy device queries the directory server and implements a policy transaction protocol. Since the device communicates directly with the policy server via a policy transaction protocol, the policy server is not required to translate and does not need the assistance of a policy proxy for the push function.

Figure 6.6 is an example where the network administrator has installed a policy in the directory server that states: "Lynne may run her video application only during nonbusiness hours." The active policy device in this example is a next-generation router executing the COPS or DIAMETER protocol

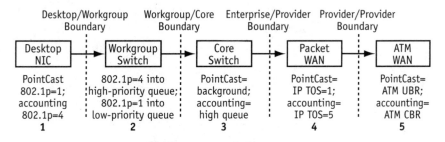

Desktop/Workgroup Boundary	Workgroup/Core Boundary	Enterprise/Provider Boundary	Provider/Provider Boundary	
Desktop NIC	Workgroup Switch	Core Switch	Packet WAN	ATM WAN
PointCast 802.1p=1; accounting 802.1p=4	802.1p=4 into high-priority queue; 802.1p=1 into low-priority queue	PointCast= background; accounting= high queue	PointCast= IP TOS=1; accounting= IP TOS=5	PointCast= ATM UBR; accounting= ATM CBR
1	2	3	4	5

FIGURE 6.6   Active policy device–layer 3 packet filtering

Assume that it is 2:00 p.m. on Wednesday afternoon, and Lynne attempts to launch her video application. The following describes the potential steps involved in the policy transaction. Note that the numbers in Figure 6.3 correspond to these procedural steps.

1. The router determines that the inbound packet contains video from Lynne's desktop by examining the source IP address and the application's well-known port number.
2. The COPS/DIAMETER client on the router transmits a request to the policy server asking it to determine if Lynne is authorized to run her video application.
3. Upon receipt of the COPS/DIAMETER request, the policy server utilizes LDAP to access the directory server to obtain Lynne's user profile.
4. The policy server also utilizes the Network Time Protocol to access the time server to obtain the time-of-day/date.
5. After the directory and time servers respond, the policy interpreter makes a policy decision and formulates a policy lease.
6. The policy interpreter transmits the policy lease to the router via the COPS/DIAME-TER protocol.

7. After receiving the policy decision, the router constructs a packet filter that blocks Lynne's video traffic until 5:00 p.m.

Active Policy Device: Desktop CoS

This example shows the operation of an active policy node that does not implement a policy transaction protocol because the requester, interpreter, and enforcer functions execute on the same node. Since the interaction between the interpretation function and the enforcement function is internal to the device, it is irrelevant to the overall transaction if the device implements a policy transaction protocol or a set of internal APIs.

Figure 6.7 shows an example in which a legacy application that is unaware of the node's traffic prioritization capabilities initiates a video-conferencing session on the application's well-known port.

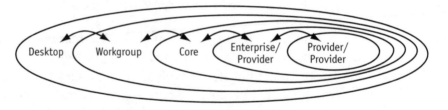

FIGURE 6.7   Active policy device: Destop CoS

The following list describes the possible steps involved in the policy transaction. The numbers in Figure 6.6 correspond to these procedural steps.

1. The service request causes the local enforcing agent to request a policy decision via an internal API from the local policy interpreter so the enforcer can assign the appropriate 802.1p/IP ToS priority values.

2. Upon receipt of the request from the enforcer, the interpreter issues an LDAP query to the directory server to retrieve the application port-to-802.1p/IP ToS mappings. In the meantime, the interpreter could return a locally stored default permission, such as sending the traffic "best-effort" or even sending it at a better service level but marking it for early discard in the event of network congestion.

3. The directory service responds with application port-to-802.1p/IP ToS mappings via LDAP.
4. After the directory service responds, the local interpreter formulates a policy lease.
5. The interpreter instructs the enforcer of the values to assign to the packets 802.1p and IP ToS fields via the internal API.

Passive Policy Device: Modify Default Queue Mapping

Passive policy device implements a policy transaction protocol but may be too busy forwarding traffic to issue queries to a policy server. In this example, the enforcement device relies on a policy proxy to send it notification of policy change from the policy server. In Figure 6.8, the passive policy device is a Layer 2 switch executing a COPS/DIAMETER client. Assume that the network administrator has decided to modify the default network policy by assigning all traffic arriving with an 802.1p Priority = 5 to the highest-priority queue (Queue 4) rather than to the second-highest- priority queue (Queue 3).

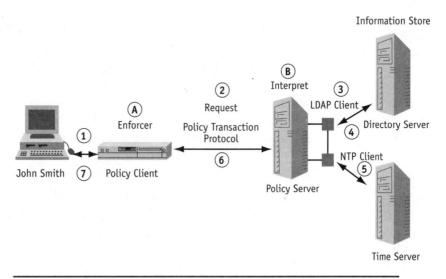

FIGURE 6.8 Passive policy device: Modify default priority-to-queue mapping

For this implementation framework, the switch does not query the policy server with each packet arrival, since this would have a severely detrimental impact on the switch's forwarding performance. In the absence of queries, the following list describes the likely steps involved in a policy transaction to inform the Layer 2 switch that the policy has been changed. The letters and numbers in Figure 6.8 correspond to these procedural steps.

A. The policy proxy constantly monitors those elements of the policy information set that pertain to the Layer 2 switch. The policy proxy pretends to be the enforcer and periodically queries the policy interpreter to determine the switch's policy.

B. Alternatively, the policy interpreter could monitor the management interface and inform the policy proxy whenever a policy has been changed that affects one of its client nodes.

1. Independent of the method employed by the policy proxy to learn that the policy has changed, the policy proxy pushes an unsolicited response via COPS/DIAMETER to inform the enforcement node of the policy change.

2. Upon receipt of this notification from the policy proxy, the enforcer transmits a COPS/DIAMETER request to the policy server to retrieve the new policy configuration.

3. Upon receipt of the COPS/DIAMETER request, the policy server utilizes LDAP to access the directory server to obtain the policy changes.

4. The directory server utilizes LDAP to respond to the policy server's request.

5. After the directory server responds, the policy interpreter makes a policy decision and formulates a policy lease.

6. The policy proxy pushes the policy lease to the Layer 2 switch via the COPS/DIAMETER protocol.

7. Based on the policy decision, the enforcer on the Layer 2 switch modifies its configuration so that all traffic arriving with an 802.1p Priority = 5 is assigned to the highest-priority queue (Queue 4), rather than to the second-highest-priority queue (Queue 3).

Organizations that take the time to deploy a network capable of supporting directory-enabled device configuration management and policy-powered networking can realize significant benefits:

✦ Network administrators no longer have to configure individual network nodes in a box-by-box manner. Device configuration is performed by manipulating the global directory service. A single change to the directory can modify the configuration of hundreds or possibly thousands of network nodes.

✦ The evolution to a standardized schema simplifies the complex task of device configuration in a multivendor environment. For example, when a generic router schema is defined, all routers from all vendors will have the same user interface.

✦ Backup, replication, and synchronization of network configuration files are automatically performed by the directory service.

✦ Network maintenance costs can be reduced because the person performing device installation no longer needs to be a technical expert who understands everything about network operations. However, experienced network administrators will still be needed to configure the directory servers.

✦ Since the desktop configuration, access rights, and other policies are stored in the directory service and not on the PC's hard drive, a user always receives the same network and application configuration regardless of attachment point to the network. This means that nomadic and traveling users have a consistent experience every time they access network.

✦ The larger the network, the more difficult it is to configure and manage. This means that the greatest benefit of deploying a policy-powered network will be realized in large network environments where these benefits are needed the most.

✦ Centralized end-to-end policy management ensures that business objectives are being met in a reliable and consistent manner via automatic enforcement mechanisms in the network.

CHAPTER **7**

Understanding
Quality of Service

Businesses have economic needs to merge multiple independent networks. Running separate data, telephone, and perhaps teleconferencing networks is expensive. Applications in a multiservice environment, such as data, voice, and video, have different QoS requirements. Figure 7.1 provides an overview of such services.

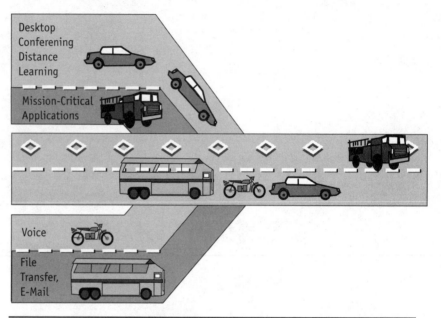

FIGURE 7.1 What is quality of service? *Source: Cisco's Erik Gilbert "End-End QoS"*

QoS provides network services that are differentiated by their level of security, bandwidth, delay, jitters, error rates, cost, compression, and other parameters. Currently, there is a great deal of work under way on the protocols and products that make internetwork quality of service possible. Sections later in this chapter discuss some of these QoS parameters.

For example, delivery of real-time multiservice applications such as videoconferencing must be on time or it becomes useless. Without proper planning and configuration in a multiservice environment, other traffic can consume all the available bandwidth; there would not be enough bandwidth to allow consistent quality of service for the multiservice applications.

What Is QoS?

QoS is the guarantee a network makes to an application in terms of providing a certain contracted level of service throughout the application session. QoS is often seen as a user requirement, but the user never has any say or influence on it. Most often, when a user subscribes to a network multimedia communication service, all the service characteristics and configuration are fixed. There is not much the user can do at this point. At the Open System Interconnection (OSI) network and transport-layer protocols allow limited signaling of QoS requirements, but in practice they offer little more than the ability to choose throughput classes when X.25 is used.

TIP

OSI is a standard reference model for how messages are to be transmitted in a point-to-point telecommunication network. Its purpose is to guide product developers and implementers so that their products will consistently work with other products. The reference model defines seven layers of functions that take place at each end of a communication.

Multimedia applications, for instance, can differ enormously in their requirements for throughput and transit delay, but may need to share communications channels. Industrial process control traffic has extremely stringent requirements for delivery within known time-windows, and will often need to use the same LANs as other traffic. So the demand is growing for users to be able to state or negotiate the QoS they need *dynamically*, which will allow the infrastructure to meet their needs and meet them efficiently. QoS has become a hot topic.

Figure 7.2 shows an overview of QoS provisions for IP traffic, which are mainly to support real-time services and establish a differentiation of customers.

Much of the work on the dynamic treatment of QoS is still at the research stage, in industry and universities. Most conference programs now have a slot for QoS. QoS mechanisms are being developed for time-critical communications, the Internet, multimedia communications, and so on.

A group in ITU-T and ISO/IEC is attempting to help in all this by developing common concepts and terminology (so that not everything is called a QoS parameter), and by providing a central place where QoS methods and mechanisms can be published.

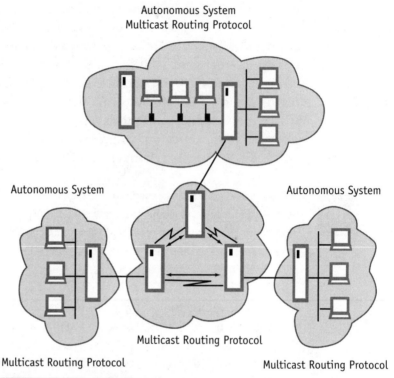

FIGURE 7.2 QoS provisions

QoS is a networking concept that resolves conflicting traffic requirements wherever voice, video, and data traffic cross paths. Without QoS, the theory goes, network congestion induces anarchy among applications, each gobbling whatever bandwidth it can.

Today, it is common for a business to rely on separate networks for data, telephone, and in some cases, videoconferencing. The high costs associated with this approach create a strong economic push to integrate all of these applications onto a single network. Among the challenges that this integration scheme presents is the fact that different types of applications have different service requirements. Finding an economical means of extending networks to support integrated services while addressing the differing needs of data, voice, and video applications will drive the success of networking in the next five years.

Network backbones need to support QoS protocols so that routers and switches can handle intensive, time-sensitive traffic loads. QoS provides network services that are differentiated by their level of security, bandwidth, delay (latency), jitters, error rates, cost, compression, and other parameters. In addition QoS techniques define ways for these different traffic types to share paths harmoniously within an internetwork. These traffic types include Constant Bit Rate (CBR) applications and Variable Bit Rate (VBR) applications.

Data, voice, and video have different QoS requirements. Real-time multimedia applications, such as videoconferencing, impose requirements on an internetwork because the traffic they produce must be delivered on a certain schedule or it becomes useless. Unlike traditional "best-effort" data services, such as File Transfer Protocol (FTP), Simple Mail Transfer Protocol (SMTP), or X Windows, in which variations in latency often go unnoticed; video and audio data are useful only if delivered within a specified time period. Later delivery only impedes the usefulness of other information within the stream. QoS protects mission-critical applications, guaranteeing its delivery and integrity, as shown in Figure 7.3

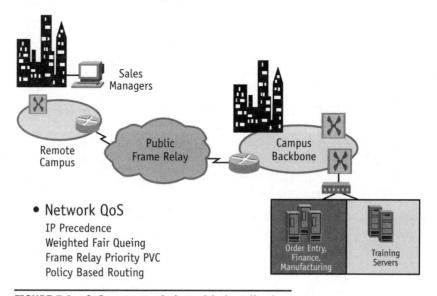

FIGURE 7.3 QoS protects mission-critical applications

Without proper network planning and configuration, the specific bandwidth needs of multimedia applications can crowd out other traffic by reducing available bandwidth, or other traffic can absorb all available bandwidth, not saving enough to allow consistent quality of service for the multimedia applications. Before network managers can create a peaceable domain wherein all internetwork flows can efficiently commingle, they must gain an understanding of the different types of flows their networks must support. Figure 7.4 depicts this scenario.

Type	Service Elements	Control Elements	Enforce Control
Quality of Service	• Classic definition of QoS • Guarantee specific services • Best efforts	• Bandwidth • Latency • Jitter • Loss of traffic	• Policy control elements
Quality of Service	• Differentiated or prioritized service levels • Best efforts	• Priority of traffic	• Policy control elements

FIGURE 7.4   Factors such as real-time interaction and multipoint distribution can affect the quality-of-service requirements for different applications

A Word About Flow

A *flow* is a distinguishable stream of related datagrams that results from a single user activity; all datagrams require the same QoS. All datagrams in a flow have the same source and destination address. For example, a flow might consist of one transport connection or one video stream between a given host pair.

Flows are simplex; they have a single source but N destinations. The flow communicates the QoS reservation requirements to the network through a flow spec that is part of the flow. Resources Reservation Protocol (RSVP) provides receiver-initiated setup of resource reservations for multicast or unicast data flows.

Put another way, a flow is a distinguishable stream of related datagrams that results from a single user activity and requires unvarying QoS. For example, a flow might consist of one transport connection or one video stream between a given host pair.

As defined by RFC 1363[1], a flowspec is a data structure that internetwork hosts use to request special service of the internetwork. Typically such special services are requests for guarantees about how the internetwork is to handle some of the hosts' traffic. Multimedia applications, frequently require hosts along the Internet path to be able to provide guarantees about the quality of the communication between applications. Minimum bandwidth requirements to ensure timely delivery of images are an example.

TIP

A *flow* is a sequence of messages that have the same source, destination (one or more), and quality-of-service requirements. Applications that generate real-time traffic have very specific quality-of-service requirements, which are communicated to the network through a flow specification.

The ATM Forum defines quality of service as a collection of the following parameters:

✦ **Rate:** The desired bite rate or bandwidth, the size of the pipe that the application wants to use

✦ **Latency:** The delay encountered by a packet, the sum of transmission delay, processing delays, which includes router look-ups, queuing delay, etc.

✦ **Jitter:** A variation of latency

✦ **Loss Ratio:** The percentage of packets dropped or lost during end-to-end transmission

✦ **Error Ratio:** The percentage of packets received in error.

NOTE

On a more intuitive level, QoS represents quantities like how fast data can be transferred, how much the receiver has to wait, how correct the received data are likely to be, how much data is likely to be lost, etc. There is no other format definition for QoS.

---

1 RFC 1363 Partridge, C., "A Proposed Flow Specification" September 1992.

Two of the most important parameters are latency and jitter, as they directly affect the quality of service. We should look at each one of them.

Latency

Many real-time interactive applications are sensitive to accumulated delay. A round-trip latency budget (round-trip delay) of less than 400 ms is quite common. The sending computer, the network, and the receiving computer all contribute to the round-trip latency budget.

Most internetworking devices receive a packet before sending it out on another interface. Referred to as processing delay, the amount of delay that the device introduces depends on:

✦ The size of the packet
✦ The speed of the media
✦ The processing steps the device might have to perform, which can include:
  ✧ Looking up a route and changing a header
  ✧ Changing the data-link layer encapsulation
  ✧ Incrementing the hop count.

The network introduces latency with the types of delay shown in Table 7.1.

TABLE 7.1   Network Induced Latency

Delay Type	Description
Propagation	Amount of time it takes information to travel the distance of the line. The speed of light controls propagation delay. Propagation delay is independent of the networking technology used.
Transmission	Amount of time it takes to put a packet on the media. The speed of the media and the size of the packet determine the transmission delay.
Store-and-forward	Amount of time it takes for an internetworking device to receive a packet before it can send it. Examples of such devices include switches, bridges, and routers.

Jitter

Jitter can occur in networks that produce variable latency for different packets. Jitter is any inconsistency in the rate at which digital information is converted into an analog signal. Technically jitter is the abrupt and unwanted variation of one or more signal characteristics, such as the interval between successive pulses, the amplitude of successive cycles, or the frequency or phase of successive cycles.

Role of Quality of Service

Quality of service is concerned with quantities like throughput, transit delay, reliability, and so on. These are termed QoS characteristics. In any given environment, a particular set of QoS characteristics is important, and for those QoS characteristics various QoS requirements will be expressed, in terms of targets to be attained, operating ranges to be supported, etc. Information about these requirements needs to be exchanged between system elements, as do other types of information, so that the QoS can be managed. Such information is communicated between elements in QoS parameters.

The Internet, as originally conceived, offers only a very simple QoS, point-to-point best-effort data delivery. Therefore, Braden, Clark, and Shenker in RFC 1633[2] propose an extension to the Internet architecture to provide integrated support for real-time and non-real-time QoS which provides some control over end-to-end packet delays.

In addition to real-time QoS, RFC 1633 discusses establishing controlled link sharing. Controlled link sharing includes the ability to share the bandwidth on a particular link and to divide traffic into administrative classes. The classes could represent different user groups or different protocol families. RFC 1633 uses the term integrated services (IS) for an Internet service model that includes best-effort service, real-time service, and controlled link sharing.

The QoS framework aims to provide a consensus set of concepts and terminology that will enable all those developing QoS specifications to adopt common approaches, to benefit from others' work and

---

2 RFC 1633 Braden, R., Clark, D., and Shenker, S. "Integrated Services in the Internet Architecture: an Overview," June 1994.

to communicate effectively. To do this, it brings the results of liaison and consultation with a number of organizations working on QoS into one central publication intended for use as a consistent reference for QoS. Its scope is all forms of interaction between elements of systems that need to work together in order to meet user requirements for QoS.

The framework defines a number of fundamental QoS terms and some common QoS characteristics. It identifies various phases of QoS activity and the types of QoS mechanism that are appropriate in the different phases. It defines in some detail the types of QoS agreements that can be reached, and discusses the elements of QoS negotiation in peer-to-peer and multi-peer interactions. It also discusses issues relating to conformance claims.

"Traffic control" is the name given to the router function that creates different qualities of service. Three components, shown in Table 7.2, implement traffic control: the packet scheduler, the classifier, and admission control.

TABLE 7.2 Components of Traffic Control

Component	Function
Packet Scheduler	Manages the forwarding of different packet streams using a set of queues and perhaps other mechanisms like timers.
Classifier	For the purpose of traffic control and accounting, maps the incoming packet into a class based upon the contents of the existing packet header and additional classification number that may be added to each packet. A class is an abstraction local to a particular router. Different routers along the path might classify the same packet differently.
Admission Control	Implements the decision algorithm that a router or host uses to determine whether a new flow can be granted the requested QoS without having an impact on earlier guarantees.

Routers need to be able to reserve resources to provide special QoS for specific user packet streams or flows. This means routers need a flow-specific state. This represents a fundamental change to the Internet model that is based on the concept that all flow-related state should be in the end systems.

The Resources Reservation Protocol (RSVP) has been designed to meet these requirements. It specifies how the flow state added to the routers for resource reservation can be made "soft", to preserve the robustness of the Internet protocol suite.

Quality of Service Characteristics

QoS characteristics are defined by framework, which groups them into broad categories of system requirement. It also identifies two ways in which characteristics may be defined. The first one should be to specialize an abstract definition. For example, an abstract definition of transit delay may be specialized by specifying the points between which the delay is defined and by specifying the particular data units to which it applies.

Obviously any real application of QoS will need to be made concrete in this way, but for some purposes, such as defining general-purpose mechanisms, it may be better to use more abstract (or generic) characteristics. The second characteristic definition is to apply statistical functions such as mean and variance.

Managing Quality of Service

The QoS framework has management phases for given activities, where it discusses the types of requirements and mechanisms needed in each phase. The phases are:

+ **Prediction phase:** Before the interaction starts
+ **Establishment phase:** Initiating the activity itself, or re-establishing the QoS requirements and mechanisms in response to changing circumstances
+ **Operational phase:** During the course of the activity.

An important activity performed during the establishment phase is reaching agreement on the QoS that is to be supported. For each QoS characteristic concerned, this may involve determining:

+ Type of agreement that is to be reached
+ Whether resources are to be allocated to the activity
+ Whether the QoS actually achieved is to be monitored

✦ Actions to be performed if the agreed QoS could not be maintained.

Multimedia applications can be divided into three different types of traffic, as shown in Figure 7.5:

✦ **Constant Bit Rate Applications:** Audio traffic and video codecs constantly introduce bit rate traffic into networks. These applications require a minimum amount of bandwidth, and have an application-specific requirement. Figure 7.6 illustrates this condition.

✦ **Variable Bit Rate Applications:** Traditional interactive data applications, such as Telnet sessions, and interactive multimedia applications, modern codecs and LAN TV, are more "bursty" in nature and fluctuate between low and high bandwidth requirements. Figure 7.7 illustrates this condition.

✦ **Available Bit Rate Applications:** Traditional data applications, such as file transfers, and new applications, multimedia mail and multimedia notes, can function with a wide range of available bandwidth. These applications require little bandwidth to function slowly and run faster as they have access to more bandwidth. Traditional packet-switched data networks can adequately support available bit rate applications with best-effort quality-of-service guarantees. Figure 7.8 illustrates this condition.

✦ **Unspecified Bit Rate or UBR:** Non-interactive applications, like FTP and MIME mail.

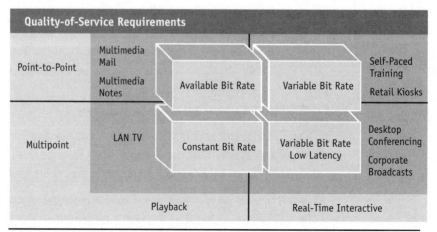

FIGURE 7.5 Multimedia applications can be divided into different types of traffic

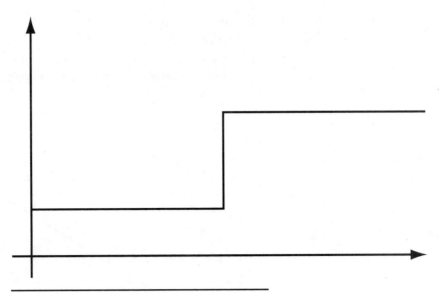

FIGURE 7.6   Constant bit rate application diagram

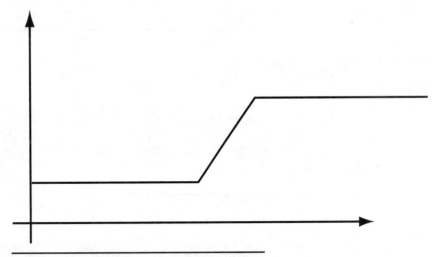

FIGURE 7.7   Variable bit rate application diagram

Circuit-switched networks are engineered to provide enough bandwidth in each circuit or virtual circuit to handle the *peak* rate required by the variable bit rate application. When the variable bit rate traffic is below the peak rate, the extra bandwidth goes unused.

Conversely, packet-switched networks provide enough bandwidth to handle two to four times the average rate required by the set of variable bit rate applications that are running. Peaks are handled by statistical sharing of the extra bandwidth, a technique known as *predictive quality of service*. Figure 7.9 provides an outline of the classes of service, which will be discussed later in this chapter.

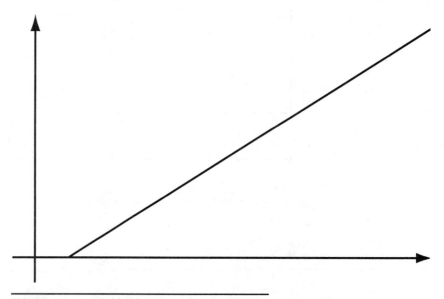

FIGURE 7.8   Available bit rate application diagram

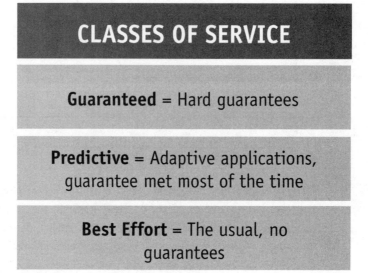

FIGURE 7.9   Classes of service outline

Quality of Service Challenges

One of the main challenges faced by quality of service mechanisms is to help control congestion, prioritize traffic, and ensure bandwidth availability. Without QoS, video, audio, and other interactive applications can block mission-critical applications from communicating or allow the network (intranets and extranets included) to become congested and slow, which could make it unpredictable and useless. Not every switch vendor is prepared to respond to such demands. Figure 7.10 provides an overview. Cisco's QoS today provides one of the latest technologies with Catalyst 5000 and LightStream 1010 switches, as shown in Figure 7.11.

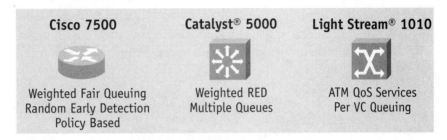

FIGURE 7.10   Quality of service challenges. *Source: Cisco's Erik Gilbert "End-End QoS"*

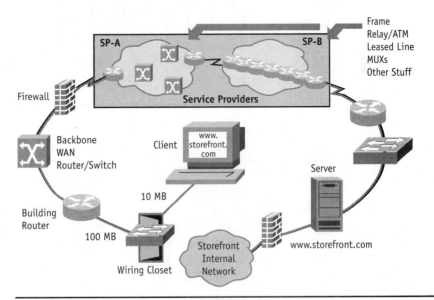

FIGURE 7.11   Cisco's QoS technology: Catalyst 5000 and Lightstream 1010 switches

A good way to understand the challenges QoS addresses and faces is to ask why we need QoS:

+ IP offers only a best-effort model of service
+ TCP guarantees reliability and sequence
+ TCP uses reactive congestion control
+ No guarantees can be made to real-time and multimedia traffic
+ Without QoS the network has to guarantee some level of quality of service.

As DEN becomes more familiar and vendors begin to implement the technology, QoS mechanisms will become even more critical. Actually, I believe the implementation of QoS mechanisms will coincide with the deployment of DEN. The QoS mechanisms being developed today will apply to all versions of Ethernet from 10 and 100 to 1000 mbit/s. The spread of DEN implementation and QoS is complementary. Figure 7.12 provides an overview of QoS in the role of directories.

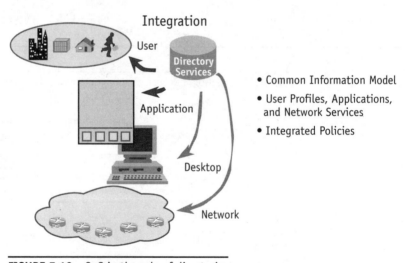

FIGURE 7.12   QoS in the role of directories

I believe DEN will require greater bandwidth, especially as congestion over the Internet grows; this will demand the prioritization and bandwidth reservation elements of QoS. In fact, QoS is becoming an increasingly essential part of the network paradigm, prioritizing applications, as shown in Figure 7.13. Figure 7.14 shows Cisco's model for QoS integration with DEN.

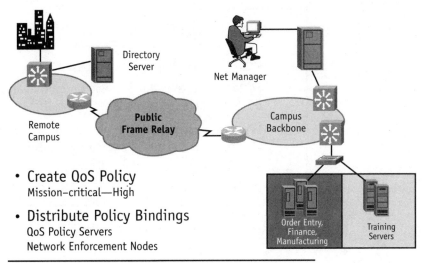

- **Create QoS Policy**
  Mission–critical—High

- **Distribute Policy Bindings**
  QoS Policy Servers
  Network Enforcement Nodes

FIGURE 7.13   QoS enables the prioritization of applications.

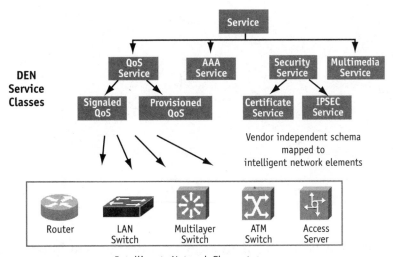

FIGURE 7.14   QoS integration with DEN

When we look at the challenges QoS faces, there are two types of basic service to consider: class of service (CoS) and QoS. Figure 7.15 shows a view of the service, control, and enforce elements. Figure 7.16 provides a QoS provision.

> → Qos provisions for IP traffic is a MUST
>   ✓ Support for real-time services
>   ✓ Differentiation of customers
>
> → Scalable solutions for provisioning and maintenance
>   of routes of guaranteed Qos to IP traffic
>
> → IP-centric approaches
>   ✓ Reservation capabilities to the routers
>
> → ATM-centric approaches
>   ✓ Map traffic sources to CBR, VBR, ABR, UBR

FIGURE 7.15   Types of QoS mechanisms and attributes

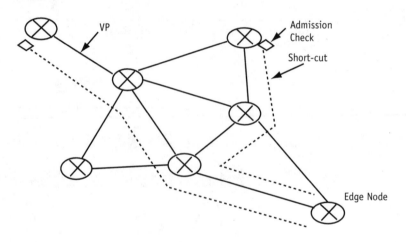

FIGURE 7.16   QoS provisions

Potential Issues in Implementing a QoS System in DEN

Some of the issues to be addressed when implementing QoS for DEN
are:

+ Congestion control
+ Admission control
+ Reservation of resources
+ QoS specification
+ QoS mapping

◆ Policing–Rate control
◆ Policing–Scheduling

These issues are discussed in greater detail in Chapter 8.

Class of Service

The class of service defines the type of traffic that is divided into several differentiated levels of priority. CoS implies differentiated classes of services, as shown in Figure 7.17, such as traffic flows originating from various types of applications on the network. Video-conference, for instance, gets priority during company-wide broadcasts, or best effort e-mail gets priority over non-critical printing jobs, and so on. Figure 7.18 justifies CoS.

➤ Traffic lows are characterized in terms of CoS (Class of Service)

➤ CoS
    ✓ Bw characteristics
    ✓ Performance characteristics
    ✓ Others (protocol, priority, etc.)

➤ CoS attributes MUST be managed and guaranteed
    ✓ Performance target associated with each attribute

➤ The notion of CoS compatible with known traffic types (more general)

FIGURE 7.17 An overview of CoS

➤ Discreet nature
  ✓ Mapping
  ✓ Comparison

➤ Partitions the space of QoS from the network
  perspectives

➤ Network planning—resource dimensioning
  ✓ Solvable
  ✓ ...but challenging

➤ Scales to multiple providers
  ✓ Discreet ranges

FIGURE 7.18   Reasons for CoS

CHAPTER 8

Directory-Based QoS Management

While widely discussed for database, multimedia, or ATM-based systems, QoS management problems in DEN are still being developed. As an important part of DEN, QoS directory-based management plays a crucial role in its total success.

QoS metrics can be applicable for Web-based systems: a number of system controllable parameters, mechanisms, QoS models, and management policies can be employed at different stages of Web service management.

QoS Models

There are two QoS models:

✦ Reservation model: Such as RSVP, ATM, etc.
  ✧ Signaling of service requests through network
  ✧ Switch/Router based per-flow queuing
✦ Precedent/Priority/Differential model
  ✧ Packet is market
  ✧ Switch/Router fabric preferentially handles packet based on markings.

The QoS models enable service providers to integrate the two service models and use the advantages of both. Network QoS is a subject that involves both network devices and routers. Consider one of the leading technologies available from Cisco.

Cisco Net*Works* software provides sufficient QoS for real-time Internet applications, and also enjoys the support of 80 percent of the routers on the Internet. For example, a service provider can implement RSVP at the edge of the network and use QoS for core routers, as shown in Figure 8.1

Cisco Net*Works* software includes the RSVP client library, which allows Internet devices to request guaranteed bandwidth for their applications. Cisco Net*Works* software also supports the IP QoS differentiated service model.

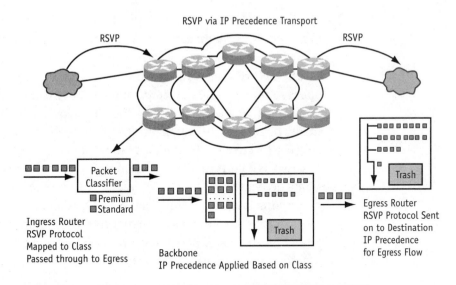

FIGURE 8.1   Mixed use of RSVP and IP precedence Quality of Service

Management Services

Internet devices require a variety of management services, depending on their function and how they interoperate on the network. Cisco's NFT supplies two broad categories of management services for Internet appliances and devices. For devices that need to be managed remotely by network administrators, NFT provides a remote management API. Some classes of appliances may need a way to discover or advertise application-level services to other devices on the network. To support this, a component of the NFT is a service location protocol. These management services are covered below.

Remote Appliance Management

For initial deployment, SNMP v2 and v3 are provided for management of devices and services. SNMP is an object-oriented remote network management protocol that is the current industry standard for network management. Components of Cisco NFT will be built with standardized APIs for remote management. Support for all core

IETF Management Information Bases (MIBs) is provided. This standardized NFT management API framework will be extensible and available for addition of partner-specific functionality.

The SNMP registry module provides a uniform interface for developers to manage the device through SNMP. It hides the complexity of SNMP and at the same time allows the devices to be managed easily through higher-level applications such as Hypertext Transfer Protocol (HTTP) or Java Dynamic Management Kit (JDMK).

Cisco NFT offers a set of common command and control components dedicated to the management of IP appliances. These programmatic interfaces allow for a generic "vocabulary" of commands common across all devices, irrespective of the specific function the device performs. The management APIs included in Cisco's NFT include functions to perform the following tasks:

✦ Starting, stopping, and rebooting
✦ Loading a new boot image
✦ Loading and resetting authorization information
✦ Loading and modifying service location information
✦ Retrieving generic performance statistics
✦ Configuring NFT services
✦ Configuring application-specific services
✦ Retrieving accounting statistics
✦ Performing resource allocation.

The APIs are open and extensible. This feature allows the appliance developer to add appliance-specific management functionality to the common framework, using the existing infrastructure supplied by the NFT. Because the server-side APIs reside on the device itself, functionality of these APIs, as well as that of the device, can be upgraded or gracefully degraded dynamically over the network without bringing down the appliance or its services, as shown in Figure 8.2

The NFT reference management tool allows the administrative user to scan the local command domain for present devices, returning their service characteristics and operational statistics. A "command domain" is a group of services/appliances over which a system administrator has command and control. Compliant services/devices are those that have fully implemented the framework API. Noncompliant device information is returned on a device-by-device, best-effort basis. Figure 8.3 provides an overview of QoS components.

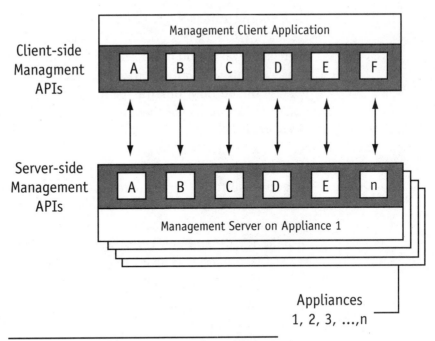

FIGURE 8.2 NFT appliance management architecture

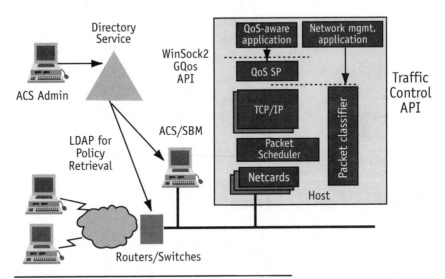

FIGURE 8.3 QoS components and integration with DEN

Unlike traditional QoS models, such as Integrated Services, which provides end-to-end guarantees on a per flow basis, Differential Services or DiffServ models are intended to provide service differentiation among traffic aggregates over large spatial granularity. As a result, in DiffServ it is possible to specify QoS requirements over the aggregate web traffic of a user, or over the entire traffic received or sent by all users of an organization, such as at Carnegie Mellon University. In addition, in DiffServ the service is defined over long time scales, rather than over the duration of a flow, as in Intserv.

Usually, DS models employ a service profile between each customer (user) and the Internet Service Provide (ISP), which defines the commitment of the ISP to the user. Unfortunately, since the set of active sources/destinations from/to, which the user sends/receives data cannot be predicted accurately at the time the service profile is associated to the user, it is very hard, if not impossible to provide fixed bandwidth profile, and simultaneously achieve high service assurance, and high resource utilization.

Two major host QoS policy components, should be outlined:

+ QoS service provider
  ✦ RSVP signaling
    – Signals service requests to network elements
    – User identity is carried in the signaling
    – IPSec integration
  ✦ Admission Control Service (ACS)/SBM Client
+ Marking based on Service Type
  ✦ IP Marking
+ Priority market in IP precedence bits
+ RSVP can be used to signal both IntServ and DiffServ service types
  ✦ Map service type to 802.1 protocol.

Admission Control Services

This section takes Microsoft's Windows operating system QoS technology as a paradigm[1], since it allows network managers to deploy QoS applications across IP and other networks. QoS APIs allow applications to invoke Admission Control Services (ACS), RSVP sig-

---

1 Based on Microsoft's white paper "Windows Quality of Service Technology", found at URL **http://www.microsoft.com/ntserver/windowsnt5/ techdetails/prodarch/winquality.asp**.

naling protocol and traffic control from Windows operating systems and the networks to which they are attached.

The ACS provide policy-based criteria when approving/denying resource requests, plus Subnet Bandwidth Measurement (SBM) functionality, to prevent bandwidth overcommitment on shared segments. RSVP provides a mechanism for conveying application QoS requirements and user identities end-to-end through the network. QoS functionality is further extended through support of traffic shaping, IP precedence, 802.1p, and varied Layer 2 media support. This gives network managers the ability to deploy QoS applications while protecting network bandwidth, and allows ISVs to use these APIs to obtain the quality they need for QoS-enabled applications

Microsoft plans to introduce, within the Windows 2000 timeframe, a QoS technology that will support the Microsoft 2000 family as well as Windows 98 operating systems. This technology will allow network managers to take advantage of a new generation of media-rich and mission-critical applications, while retaining control of network utilization. ISVs can take advantage of these APIs to obtain better network service for their mission-critical or streaming applications.

Windows QoS is especially important, because the increasing bandwidth available with Fast Ethernet and emerging Gigabit Ethernet networks has encouraged development and deployment of video-streaming, real-time audio, video conferencing, interactive communication, and other bandwidth-hungry applications that require low-latency delivery. In addition, many mission-critical applications that are not multimedia intensive still require robust QoS guarantees.

Windows QoS integrates the IETF RSVP and other elements to provide the kind of QoS that might otherwise be associated only with end-to-end asynchronous transfer mode (ATM) networks. In addition, Windows QoS can operate over a heterogeneous network topology, which includes, for example, Ethernet and ATM.

Windows QoS goes beyond facilitating media-rich delivery to providing network managers with complete control over how their bandwidth is used. Network managers can use Windows QoS to:

♦ Prevent non-adaptive protocols (such as UDP) from abusing network resources

✦ Partition resources between "best-effort" traffic and higher- or lower-priority traffic
✦ Reserve resources for entitled users
✦ Prioritize access to resources based on users.

Windows 2000 Server QoS technology allows policy-based QoS management so that bandwidth can be allocated; for example, evenly across all departments during a defined time period or preset as needed to prioritize traffics. This ensures that applications requiring QoS delivery are given the bandwidth they need, without exceeding administrator-defined bandwidth limitations.

Windows QoS also supports application-based QoS, so an administrator-defined bandwidth can be allocated to mission-critical applications such as overnight inventory or banking transactions.

Windows QoS supports:

✦ **Admission Control Services:** For allocation of network resources based on topology, resource availability, and policy regarding specific users or applications
✦ **RSVP:** The IETF-defined signaling protocol, which enables the sender and receiver in a communication session to request resources and communicate policy information to the shared network and to their peer
✦ Kernel traffic control:
  ✧ Traffic policing, shaping, and packet sequencing (including audio latency reduction on slow links)
  ✧ Control of IP precedence bits for specifying a priority level to Layer 3 devices in the network
  ✧ 802.1p prioritization for specifying a priority level to Layer 2 devices in the network
  ✧ Translation between Layer 3 QoS signaling (such as RSVP) and Layer 2 QoS signaling, for example, from RSVP to ATM.

The Windows 2000 implementation of QoS is robust and easily enhanced by independent software vendors and independent hardware vendors (IHVs). Network managers can easily manage it.

The Winsock2 Generic Quality of Service (GQoS) API allows applications to invoke QoS without knowledge of the underlying network or the specific QoS mechanisms available in the network. Created with substantial input from ISVs, the GQoS API makes it easy to deploy multivendor QoS applications and solutions across the network. The Traffic Control Application Programming Interface (TC API) allows fine-grain access to traffic control features and permits QoS to be invoked on behalf of legacy applications. Invoked by GQoS, the QoS Service Provider (SP) provides RSVP signaling to the network and peers, provides feedback to applications, and invokes Traffic Control. The QoS SP also communicates with the ACS server to prevent overcommitment of network resources and to enforce Active Directory-based policy.

All of this combines to make Windows the ideal platform for deploying mission-critical or media-rich QoS applications, while retaining control of network utilization.

Windows QoS is significant, because it enables end-to-end quality of service over the network. The QoS SP, the Generic QoS API, and the Traffic Control API work together to invoke the QoS mechanisms appropriate for the application, the underlying media, and the network, to guarantee appropriate end-to-end QoS.

Understanding Windows QoS

The Microsoft Windows 2000 server provides a full and robust implementation of QoS technology, allowing network managers to take advantage of the power of QoS applications, while retaining control of their network bandwidth.

QoS-enabled application uses the Winsock2 GQoS interface to convey QoS requirements to the Winsock2 QoS Service Provider. The QoS SP, in turn, invokes varying QoS mechanisms appropriate for the application, the underlying media, and the network to guarantee appropriate end-to-end QoS.

Key elements of Windows 2000 Server QoS include:

✦ Admission Control Services
  ✧ Subnet bandwidth management
  ✧ Policy-based admission control services
✦ APIs
  ✧ Generic QoS API
  ✧ Traffic control API
  ✧ Policy-related APIs

- ✦ QoS Service Provider
    - ✧ RSVP signaling
    - ✧ Policy
    - ✧ Traffic control invocation
- ✦ Kernel Traffic Control
    - ✧ 802.1p
    - ✧ IP precedence
    - ✧ Traffic shaping
    - ✧ Slow links
    - ✧ Supporting additional Layer 2 QoS signaling mechanisms.

The ACS are built on the SBM platform (defined by the IETF). The SBM extends RSVP to perform simple resource-based admission control on shared segments, such as Ethernet. ACS adds the necessary functionality to perform sophisticated policy-based admission control.

Because ACS is a service, it can be enabled on any Windows 2000 server on a network and therefore does not require a separate machine on which to operate. ACS servers use the Windows 2000 Active Directory to enforce policy. Note that open policy APIs also allow third-party network equipment (such as routers and switches) to implement ACS based on the Windows 2000 Active Directory.

Subnet Bandwidth Management

A network may consist of several subnets interconnected with routers. Multiple clients and servers may use the same pool of shared bandwidth on each subnet. An SBM server limits the admission of reservations on a subnet by reviewing each bandwidth reservation request. In conformance with the IETF draft, the SBM inserts itself in the reservation path to review reservation messages to determine the availability of resources. In addition, Microsoft's ACS adds value beyond this basic admission control function by reviewing reservation messages against policies stored in directory services

Policy-Based Admission Control Services

Network managers can use policy from the Active Directory to limit the amount of traffic any individual can reserve in any particular subnet at any particular time. Administration is facilitated by the ability to apply policy to groups of users, as well as to individuals, via the use of Active Directory.

An individual user, for example, might be allowed to pull high-bandwidth video down from a local video server, but may not be allowed to pull the same video down from a video server when the traffic must traverse a backbone network. The ACS server for the backbone can reject a request by a user if the bandwidth requirement exceeds the configured limits for that user on the backbone.

Development of APIs

Windows QoS technology makes development easier for ISVs by providing the Generic QoS application programming interface (API) and the Traffic Control API.

Generic QoS API

Windows uses the GQoS API to provide an interface so designers can enable their applications to invoke QoS transparently, regardless of the underlying QoS mechanisms available.

Numerous ISVs collaborated with Microsoft in the definition of the GQoS API, and the majority of applications requiring QoS will support the GQoS API.

The GQoS API allows applications to describe the quality of service required for transmitting its data flow. The QoS parameters are carried in a generic Flowspec, as defined by the IETF Integrated Services Working Group. As an option, parameters can be handled by a provider-specific buffer to the QoS SP. Applications can use the Flowspec, which is expected to be sufficient for most applications, or exercise finer control over QoS parameters using the buffer. With either approach, the parameters are passed with existing Winsock2 calls.

Figure 8.4 illustrates the role of the GQoS API in invoking traffic control.

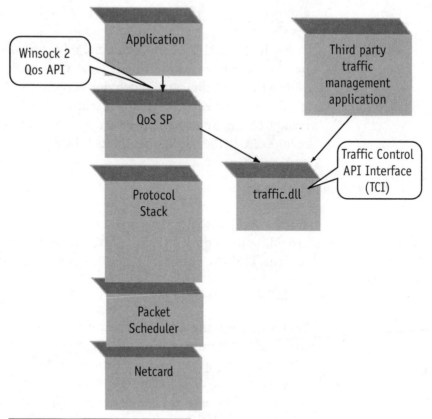

FIGURE 8.4   The QoS-enabled stack

Traffic Control API

The Traffic Control API allows third-party traffic management applications and the QoS Service Provider to invoke traffic control on behalf of applications. As noted earlier, third-party traffic management applications may be used to request traffic control on behalf of applications that are unable to do so on their own, or in situations in which a system administrator wants to control the QoS provided to applications. These applications use the Traffic Control API instead of GQoS.

In addition, the Traffic Control API allows the aggregation of traffic from a number of sources (on the same sending host) into a single traffic control flow. For example, all traffic to destination net 1.2.3.0 could be placed on the same flow, regardless of source address and port and destination port. By comparison, the Generic QoS API limits the use of a traffic control flow to traffic from a single "conversation" only (a conversation is defined by source and destination address and port).

Currently, third-party traffic management applications can only invoke traffic control on behalf of other applications (as opposed to end-to-end QoS signaling such as RSVP). A future release will provide a mechanism by which third-party applications can invoke a signaling protocol (and, by extension, traffic control) on behalf of other applications.

Creating a Flow and Adding Filters

A key element of traffic control is to establish the service parameters for a sequence of packets and then treat all members of the packet as a single flow.

Traffic control uses information from the Flowspec to create a flow with defined QoS parameters. The user of the API then creates filters to direct selected packets through this flow. The Traffic Control API also verifies that TC components have the resources available to provide the requested QoS parameters.

QoS Service Provider

Windows QoS technology includes the QoS Service Provider, which responds to the GQoS API. Part of the operating system, the QoS SP implements the RSVP signaling protocol and communicates with ACS. QoS applications can invoke its services via the Winsock2 GQoS API. The QoS SP also invokes local traffic control on behalf of applications.

RSVP Signaling

The Resource Reservation Protocol is designed to carry resource reservation requests through networks of varying topologies and media. Through RSVP, a user's quality of service requests are propagated to all RSVP-aware network devices along the data path (including admission control servers), allowing resources to be reserved from all those which are RSVP-enabled, at all network levels. This allows the network to meet the desired level of service.

The RSVP reserves network resources by establishing flows end-to-end through the network. A flow is a network path associated with one or more senders, one or more receivers, and a certain quality of service. A sending host wishing to send data requiring a certain QoS will broadcast, via the QoS Service Provider, "PATH" messages toward the intended recipients. These messages, which describe the bandwidth requirements and relevant parameters of the data to be sent, are propagated along the path.

A receiving host, interested in particular data, will reserve the resources for the flow (and the network path) by sending "RESV" messages through the network back toward the sender. As this occurs, intermediate RSVP-capable nodes, based on bandwidth capacity and policies, decide whether or not to accept the proposed reservation and commit resources. If an affirmative decision is made, the resources are committed and RESV messages are propagated to the previous hop on the path from source to destination.

Exchanging PATH and RESV Messages

At the heart of the RSVP protocol is the exchange of PATH and RESV messages with the network. The PATH message describes the QoS parameters of the traffic, the sender's address, and the destination of the traffic. The RESV message describes the QoS parameters of the traffic to be received and the source of the traffic and is sent toward the sender.

On receiving the RESV message, the QoS data flow begins. The QoS SP constructs and periodically updates the PATH and RESV messages on behalf of the application. Sending applications, such as those controlling multicast transmissions, can also be configured to begin sending immediately on a best-effort basis, which is then upgraded to QoS on receipt of the RESV message.

Verifying Admission Control

To protect network resources, the ACS decides whether to "admit" or reject a reservation request. This decision is referred to as an "admission control decision." The ACS makes admission control decisions based on the availability of resources and on policies put in place by network administrators. In its most basic form, the ACS is equivalent to the SBM. In this form, it is configured with some resource limit and views all resource requests from the network as equivalent. It admits reservations until there are no more resources to dole out.

Policy

The full ACS is also policy capable. In this form, the ACS considers parameters of the resource request, beyond the resources requested (such as the ID of the user requesting the resources). It then looks to the Active Directory to determine the policies that should be applied to the specific user. Thus, its admission control decision will be based on the availability of resources and the policies applying to the requesting user.

Scalability

The RSVP protocol, which supports both unicast and multicast reservations, is designed to scale well. For example, the reservation message from a receiver only needs to travel upstream until it reaches the first merge point in the multicast tree where resources are already reserved for this session—rather than having to return all the way to the sender.

For additional scalability, an RSVP-based enterprise can integrate well with the IP precedence used by wide-area, class-of-service–based networks. This form of aggregation of resource requests is also sometimes referred to as differentiated services. It is important to note that, by aggregating in such a manner, it is possible to realize significant QoS gains, even in networks in which only the hosts and a select few ACS nodes directly support RSVP.

Traffic Control Invocation

The QoS SP translates very abstract QoS requests from applications into specific traffic control semantics, invoking traffic control on behalf of the application and subject to availability of resources in the network (as determined by RSVP signaling).

In addition, for networks that are not RSVP-enabled, the QoS SP can be used in a pass-through mode in which it will invoke local traffic control functionality without RSVP signaling. The QoS SP invokes local traffic control via the same Traffic Control API used by third-party traffic management applications.

Kernel Traffic Control

The Traffic Control API provides fine-grain kernel traffic control for traffic policing, shaping and packet sequencing, 802.1p, IP precedence, and Layer 2 signaling (such as ATM). Kernel Traffic Control can be invoked by third-party traffic management applications to provide QoS for legacy applications.

Supporting 802.1p

Windows QoS provides support for 802.1p tags, helping to provide QoS across Layer 2 switches. Traffic control can be used to determine the 802.1p user priority value carried in the Media Access Control (MAC) header field to give relative packet priority. This tag describes, to capable devices within the Layer 2 network, the traffic class to which the packet belongs, providing a mechanism for QoS support. ACS and its policy functionality can be used to limit the creation of 802.1p prioritized flows.

IP Precedence

IP precedence provides the capability to partition traffic into multiple classes of service. Traffic control can be used to set bits in the IP headers of packets on particular flows. These bits are interpreted by Layer 3 network devices with the result that packets belonging to a flow will be treated appropriately later by devices on the network. These fields are analogous to 802.1p priority settings, but are interpreted by higher-layer network devices.

The IP Precedence feature allows policy to be used to either set or override the precedence assignment. IP precedence can be mapped into adjacent technologies (such as tag switching, frame relay, or ATM) to deliver end-to-end QoS policies in a heterogeneous network environment. Thus, IP precedence enables service classes to be established with no changes to existing applications and with no complicated network signaling requirements.

IP precedence is a key mechanism in enabling QoS to scale across large networks. Network equipment in these networks can support IP precedence (which is stateless) with less overhead than full RSVP reservations require. By using the policy functionality of ACS, it is possible to control the use of IP precedence by endstations, such that resource allocations are managed and their integrity can be maintained across these large networks.

In this manner, we can build networks that combine RSVP functionality and IP precedence (also referred to as differentiated services or class-of-service networks), to obtain end-to-end QoS guarantees. Those parts of the network that are RSVP-capable will provide true RSVP reservations. Those parts of the network that are not will support IP precedence.

Traffic Shaping

The Packet scheduler retrieves the packets and transmits them according to the QoS parameters, which generally include a scheduled rate (token bucket parameter) and some internal priority. The former is used to pace the transmission of packets to the network. The latter is used to determine the order in which queued packets should be submitted to the network when congestion occurs.

Slow Links

Special mechanisms are provided to perform traffic shaping on slow links, such as 28.8 Kbps modem links. On such links, large packets can occupy the link long enough to delay small audio packets, which must be sent on the same link. This can wreak havoc with audio quality. To avoid this problem, traffic control fragments large packets, at the link layer, sending only one fragment at a time. Latency-sensitive audio packets can then be inserted in between the larger packet's fragments, thus reducing audio latency and improving audio quality.

Supporting Additional Layer 2 Control Mechanisms

The QoS SP may invoke additional traffic control mechanisms, depending on the specific underlying data-link layer. It may signal an underlying ATM network, for instance, to set up an appropriate virtual circuit for each flow. It may also generate the appropriate signaling for cable modem networks or other Layer 2 media.

As network bandwidth increases and as mission-critical and media-rich applications such as video conferencing, shared whiteboarding, and IP telephony find a growing place in the enterprise, network managers will be able to use Windows QoS technology to deploy QoS-enabled applications without losing control of their network.

Windows QoS technology provides great opportunities for ISVs and IHVs with its Generic QoS API and Traffic Control API.

The GQoS API enables applications to invoke QoS from the QoS SP regardless of the characteristics of the underlying network. The QoS SP is integrated with the operating system to implement the RSVP signaling protocol and communicates with the Admission Control Services server to prevent overcommitment of bandwidth on shared segments. QoS functionality is extended through support of 802.1p and IP precedence.

The Traffic Control API enables third-party traffic-management applications, and the QoS SP, to invoke QoS on behalf of applications, including those unable to do so on their own or in situations in which a system administrator wants to control the QoS provided to applications.

All of this combines with the policy-based and applications-based QoS management to make Windows 2000 Server the ideal platform for deploying media-rich QoS applications, while retaining control of network utilization.

CHAPTER **9**

DEN and Network Services Security

Data security and maintaining system integrity are the primary concerns when implementing DEN. Data security can be provided by a number of security mechanisms in the operating system, as well as by communications security mechanisms. Protecting the operating system from unwanted intrusions and attacks originating from remote systems can ensure system integrity, from a networking viewpoint.

Network security can be viewed as a feature of the user's operating system, as a feature of the networking infrastructure, and/or as a networking service in which end and infrastructure components have roles. Internet Protocol Security (IPSec) is one aspect of network security, used to protect Internet Protocol (IP) packet exchanges among end-systems and network infrastructure components.

NOTE

Participants in the IETF IPSec Working Group, available at **http://www.ietf.org/ html.charters/ipsec-charter.html** have developed detailed specifications for IPSec.

Generally, network security solutions should feature the following characteristics:

+ Traffic data confidentiality, integrity, and authenticity
+ Policy-based access, authorization, and routing control
+ Guaranteed availability throughout the network
+ Temporal consistencies with respect to policy enforcement
+ Verifiable coherence with respect to policy enforcement
+ Ability to do narrow troubleshooting without compromising network security
+ Support of monitoring and auditing activities
+ Interoperation with end-systems and networking components
+ Legal compliance in the jurisdiction of deployment.

Network security service architecture can easily take advantage of DEN functions. This chapter, based on Microsoft's William Dixon's contribution, describes a policy-based approach using DEN to provide network security with IPSec. Since it seems difficult to view "IPSec" as a service in the network, we should think of IPSec transport and tunneling as capabilities of end-stations and infrastructure components. However, ISAKMP was designed to be a negotiation service. Therefore, IPSec policy is discussed in terms of being applicable to particular end-station or infrastructure components, which themselves have representative objects in the directory service. Consumers of IPSec information in the directory are:

✦ The end-system or infrastructure component to which the policy applies
✦ Management applications
✦ Potential adversaries with the intent to compromise network security.

This last point underscores the importance of product design trade-offs, deciding how much security policy to expose, to whom, and in what way.

IPSec Functions Supported

This specification should evolve to address the following types of client (clients who receive and enforce IPSec policy) functions:

✦ Locate network security components/resources, such as gateways, firewall, tunnel servers, and IPSec policy servers
✦ Discover its own machine IPSec policy, or IPSec policies of a user
✦ Discover the IPSec policy of other components.

The following types of management functions should also be addressed and facilitated by the IPSec policy mechanisms:

✦ Configuring client and component policy; add, delete, change, notification
✦ Verifying that a particular policy is in effect
✦ Access control to policy
✦ Security policy meta-data.

If an ISAKMP-based implementation of IPSec is in use, then compatibility issues, other client policy, etc. may be discovered during the negotiation of a security association.

Attributes and Classes

Care should be taken to implement directory storage of policy in a manner consistent with the needs of consumers of the information. Global availability of the policy information may not be required or desired.

Consider that one or several IPSec policies may be active in a component at any one time. Each policy would describe one model of communication, involving a number of security controls on various types of traffic, for example VPN employee policy, employee intranet policy, and vendor extranet policy. It is then desirable to allow a negotiation service such as ISAKMP to decide among a number of allowable options for securing the traffic type to some destination. Consequently, IPSec policy can be composed of eight classes:

1. **IPSec Policy Identification:** A set of attributes to describe a policy, such as an object ID, friendly name, description, owner, version, revision, and to reference its traffic rules
2. **IPSec Traffic Rules:** A means of associating filters with other component policies to secure a given traffic type
3. **IPSec Traffic Type (Filters/Selectors):** How to classify network traffic, e.g. protocols, addresses, ports, applications, users, machines, networks, interfaces, locality
4. **IPSec Security Policy:** What mechanisms for security are desired/required, including algorithms and IPSec modes
5. **IPSec ISAKMP Policy:** Attributes for ISAKMP, such as rekey times, perfect forward secrecy
6. **IPSec Authentication Policy:** What means of authentication/trust are desired/required as we establish Internet connectivity?
7. **IPSec Event Policy:** What to do for exceptions, errors, auditable events; what reporting interfaces/mechanisms to use (SNMP, e-mail, Windows Management Interface, etc.)
8. **IPSec Policy Consumer List:** Attributes list to identify that a particular consumer has been assigned this policy. Required for verification of resources to users.

By composing these classes, one can arrive at a policy model that provides a rich, flexible policy statement with which to secure a network of IP traffic. This document proposes to store IPSec policy in the directory service, where directory clients using LDAP can access it. The specification, albeit standardized, may be the lesser of the obstacles to successful deployment.

A product which is built upon this specification must have a usage model that addresses issues of administrative maintenance, such as how to represent these policy objects and relationships to the user, change notification, as well as how to handle the change of a filter, which itself is used in six rules which are components of four policies, used by 1000 clients, some of whom may be export-only versions of the product and/or remote access clients using the same directory service for policy. Consequently, a few classes are needed to enable a client to find an assigned policy.

- **IPSec Policy Store/Server:** The location to go to find the policy for the client
- **IPSec Policy Assignment:** The specific policy reference which applies for the client. This avoids having to extend the possible parent classes themselves to add the policy assignment attribute, which may itself be multivalued.

These classes are instantiated as objects located in the directory service in well-defined places so that a standard LDAP query from any client implementation can find the appropriate policy assignment. This is likely to be globally available. However, the policy assignment will likely depend upon the physical location of a client and/or a client's or user's membership in a group, or perhaps the legal constraints of the operational environment.

Base Classes Extended

A few administrative management attributes are shown in the next section as suggestions for extending the base classes. Otherwise, all the classes proposed are derived from original DEN spec base classes and subclasses that further specify the base classes.

Attributes

Only a few attributes are given in this version of the draft for clarification. The syntax can be, as shown in Table 9.1, whatever makes sense that people can agree upon. Certain attributes should be inherited from parent classes, such as Owner, Version, Revision, RevOwner, DateTime. The base classes and immediate subclasses do not presently have these attributes.

TABLE 9.1   Syntax Attributes

Name	Syntax	Description
ObjectID	String GUID	
Common Name	Unicode String	Text-friendly name of the policy
Description	Unicode String	Text description of the policy
Owner	Unicode String	Current owner of policy definition, userid@dns.name.name.name
Version	Unicode String	Software name and version stamp followed by policy version number (mgmt app specific)
Revision	Integer	Monotonically increasing revision number under the given version; start with 1. 0=delete me
RevDateTime	DateTime	Date and time that revision was made
RevOwner	Unicode String	
DataType	Integer	Type of data in class; defined by each class

Classes

This section provides concise specifications of each class used to represent IPSec policy. A few attributes are provided for illustrative purposes. In some cases improvement is needed to clarify the difference between lists of objects and the objects themselves. But the class idea, as shown in Table 9.2, should be apparent. Most attributes are shown as MUST, but this should be viewed in this draft as a recommendation. MAY attributes are listed in Table 9.3 to show possibilities.

TABLE 9.2   Class Ideas

Class	IPSecPolicyID
Description	The root object which identifies a particular IPSec policy, which will have references to component objects
OID	
Derived From	Policy::SecurityPolicy

continued on next page

Class	IPSecPolicyID
Auxiliary Classes	
Possible Superiors	Service::IPSecService::IPSecPolicies
MUST Attributes	Name, Description, IPSecTrafficRules, IPSecEventPolicy, IPSecConsumerList, IPSecPolicyStore
MAY Attributes	

TABLE 9.3 MAY Attributes

Class	IPSec Traffic Rule
Description	Describes how to protect a given traffic type using IPSec.
OID	
Derived From	Policy::SecurityPolicy
Auxiliary Classes	
Possible Superiors	IPSecPolicyID
MUST Attributes	Revision, RevDateTime, IPSecTrafficSelectors, IPSecSecurityPolicy, IPSecISAKMPPolicy

Revision and RevDateTime are included here to emphasize that Traffic Rule changes may be distinguished from entire policy changes, so that decisions on what to do when the policy components change can be fairly optimal for the clients.

Class	IPSecTrafficSelector
Description	How to classify network traffic, eg. filter specification
OID	
Derived From	Policy::SecurityPolicy
Auxiliary Classes	
Possible Superiors	IPSecTrafficRule
MUST Attributes	ProtocolID, SourceIP, SourceMask, SourcePort, DestIP, DestMask, DestPort, SelectorType
MAY Attributes	TypeOfService, Priority, TunneledProto, SourceDNSName, DestDNSName, SourceUserID, DestUserID, StartTime, EndTime, Interface, Outbound, Inbound

Class	IPSecSecurityPolicy
Description	The security method for negotiation
OID	
Derived From	Policy::SecurityPolicy
Auxiliary Classes	
Possible Superiors	IPSecTrafficRule
MUST Attributes	SecEncryptAlg, SecKeyLen, SecAuthAlg, SecKeyLen

Class	IPSecISAKMPPolicy
Description	The attribute settings to achieve a desired ISAKMP negotiation behavior and capability
OID	
Derived From	Policy::SecurityPolicy
Auxiliary Classes	
Possible Superiors	IPSecTrafficRule
MUST Attributes	MMEncryptAlg, MMEncryptKeyLen, MMKeyLifetime, QMKeyLifetime, MMPerfectForwardSecrecyOn, QMPerfectForwardSecrecyOn
MAY Attributes	UseAggressiveMode, AMEncryptAlg, AMKeyLifetime

Class	IPSecAuthenticationPolicy
Description	The methods of authentication acceptable to ISAKMP negotiation
OID	
Derived From	Policy::SecurityPolicy
Auxiliary Classes	
Possible Superiors	IPSecISAKMPPolicy
MUST Attributes	AuthType
MAY Attributes	AuthCredential

Class	IPSecEventPolicy
Description	Attributes for determining how to handle certain error, exception and audit events
OID	
Derived From	Policy::SecurityPolicy
Auxiliary Classes	
Possible Superiors	IPSecTrafficRule
MUST Attributes	IPSecEventID, EventResponseID, EventAuditSuccess, EventAuditFail

Class	IPSecPolicyConsumerList
Description	An updateable list of the objects which are currently assigned a particular IPSec policy. Necessary for propagation of changes and verification of "completeness", that every assigned system is in fact using the assigned policy. Consistency maintained by policy assignment mechanism.
OID	
Derived From	Policy::SecurityPolicy
Auxiliary Classes	
Possible Superiors	IPSecTrafficRule
MUST Attributes	ConsumerType, ConsumerID

Note that the consumer list is per IPSecTrafficRule. Choice of granularity here is to identify which consumers are protecting which traffic. It would also or instead be possible do it for IPSecPolicy. But it seems that traffic rules may be defined and incorporated into different overall policies depending on how policy assignment is done.

Class	IPSecPolicyStore, IPSecPolicyServer
Description	The place to go to for IPSec policy. Could be a policy storage location the reference to which is in a device profile, or server which provides the service referenced either in a device profile or discovered by way of the IPSecService object in the directory service.
OID	
Derived From	Policy::SecurityPolicy
Auxiliary Classes	
Possible Superiors	Protocol::NetworkProtocol::Layer3::ConnectionLess:: IP::IPSEC, or alternately Service::IPSecService:: IPSecPolicyServer.
MUST Attributes	StoreType, StoreName

Class	IPSecPolicyAssignment
Description	Specific policy object reference for a type of assignment
OID	
Derived From	Policy::SecurityPolicy
Auxiliary Classes	
Possible Superiors	Profile::UserProfile, Profile::GroupProfile, Profile::OrganizationProfile, Profile::OUProfile, Profile::ServiceProfile, Application::ApplicationProcess:: [Single|Multiple]UserApplication::<application>
MUST Attributes	ConsumerType, PolicyStoreRef, PolicyObjectRef, revision_time

Omitted here are the classes which may be used to contain the associations (1:many lists of objects) between instantiated objects. Such a class might be IPSec Rule to Policy List which is simply a list of pointers to each IPSec Traffic Rule instance that the administrator has assigned as being a component of a certain IPSecPolicyID.

Class	IPSec Rules To Policy List
Description	The way to keep track of which rules are part of a policy
OID	
Derived From	Policy::SecurityPolicy
Auxiliary Classes	
Possible Superiors	IPSecPolicyID
Must Attributes	IPSecTrafficRuleNum, IPSecTrafficRulePtr1
May Attributes	IPSecTrafficRulePtr2, ...

The diagram shown in Figure 9.1 represents the container and pointer relationships noted in the Possible Superiors row of the class specifications. The derivative relationships are not shown for IPSec policy components, but are indicated by the :: symbol for other objects. The arrows indicate pointers to other objects, not a "contained within" relationship.

Example of Use

With the policy outlined in Figure 9.1, CLIENT2 will communicate IP traffic using DES-CBC to the machine LEGAL2 using certificates to mutually authenticate end-to-end, and using CORPGATE-IPSEC as the IPSec tunnel server when dialed in to the user's ISP account from home.

CLIENT2 exists as an object in the directory service of the Device class and has a device profile of class Profile::DeviceProfile. An IPSec policy has been assigned to this device by way of a pointer reference in the Device profile to an IPSec policy object of class Policy::Security Policy:IPSecPolicyID. Alternately, CLIENT2 may receive a policy assignment in much the same way as it receives a dynamically assigned IP address, from an IPSec policy server. After receiving an IP address, it does an LDAP query to the directory service to find out the location of the IPSec policy server by querying for objects of class Service::IPSecService::IPSecPolicyServer.

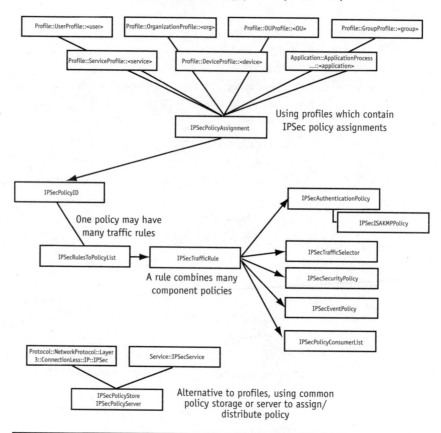

Directory Enabled Networking
Relationship of IPSec Policy Components
per IPSec DEN Draft Networking (February 16, 1998)

FIGURE 9.1   Container and pointer representations noted in the Possible Superiors
row of the class specification

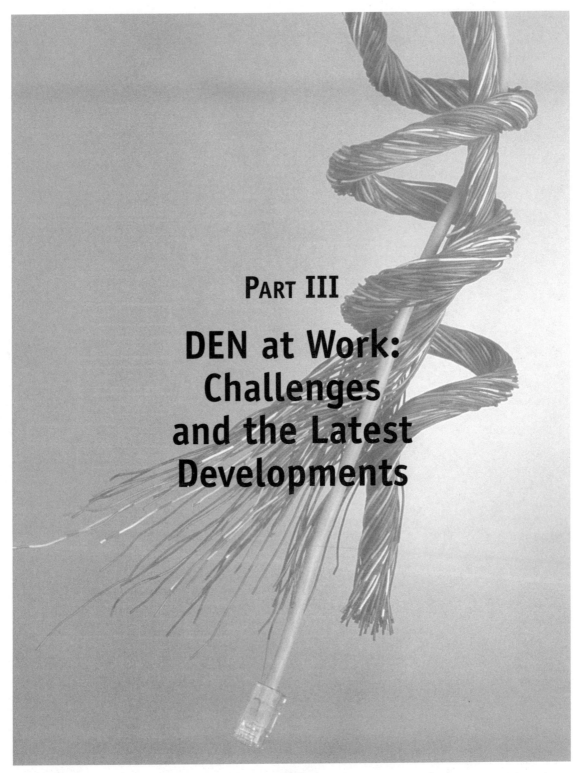

PART III

DEN at Work: Challenges and the Latest Developments

CHAPTER **10**

LDAP (v3): Dynamic Attributes for RADIUS

This chapter, based on Bernard Aboba's Internet draft, defines dynamic attributes used by the Remote Access Dialin User Service (RADIUS). These attributes are written to a dynamic directory service by the RADIUS server in order to provide information about sessions in progress. This information can then be used in order to provide for control of simultaneous logins, or for detection or tracking of security incidents in progress.

Overview

The RADIUS protocol supports authentication, authorization, and accounting for dialup users. To date, RADIUS servers have retrieved their configuration from user databases and/or flat configuration files. In order to consolidate stores of user information, it is desirable to integrate a RADIUS with an LDAP-based directory service.

This section describes how a dynamic directory service may be used to store these and other attributes relating to sessions in progress. Such information can be useful for a variety of purposes including security incident response, simultaneous usage control, or monitoring of connection quality, login time, and packet size or bandwidth usage. Because data change so frequently, dynamic attributes must be employed.

Useful attributes come from both the Access-Request and Access-Reply. For example, attributes such as Nas-IP-Address, Nas-Port, Nas-Identifier, Called-Station-ID, Calling-Station-ID, and Connect-Info are available from the RADIUS Access-Request packet. Other attributes such as Framed-IP-Address may be computed dynamically, and sent in the RADIUS Access-Accept packet. Attributes relating to a user's resource consumption during a session in progress are made available via the Interim Accounting Record Extension. These include Acct-Input-Octets, Acct-Output-Octets, Acct-Session-ID, Acct-Authentic, Acct-Session-Time, Acct-Input-Packets, Acct-Output-Packets, Acct-Terminate-Cause, Acct-Multi-Session-ID, Acct-Link-Count, Acct-Tunnel-Client-Endpoint, and Act-Tunnel-Connection-ID.

This chapter was based on an Internet draft authored by Bernard Aboba of Microsoft, entitled "LDAP (v3): Synamic Attributes for RADIUS," **< draft-aboba-dynradius-01.txt >**, November 19, 1997.

Object Definitions

The RADIUS dynamic attribute schema includes definition of a dynamic RADIUS Person class.

Dynamic RADIUS Person Class

Here it is the structure of the RADIUS Person class as defined by Aboba in his Internet draft:

```
( DynamicRadiusPersonClass 1
    NAME 'dynamicRadiusPersonClass'
    SUP top
    STRUCTURAL
    MUST (
        userName $ acctSessionId $ connectionStatus
    )
    MAY ( nasIPAddress $ nasPort $ framedIPAddress $
        class $ calledStationId $ callingStationId $
        nasIdentifier $ acctInputOctets $
        acctOutputOctets $ acctAuthentic $
        acctSessionTime $ acctInputPackets $
                acctOutputPackets $
        acctTerminateCause $ acctMultiSessionId $
                acctLinkCount $
        acctInputGigawords $ acctOutputGigawords $
        nasPortType $ tunnelType $ tunnelMediumType $
        acctTunnelClientEndpoint $ acctTunnelConnection $
        tunnelPrivateGroupId $ connectInfo $
                authenticationType $
        eapType $ encryptionType $ sessionLocalStartTime $
        sessionLocalEndTime $ ispId $ connectionStatus $
        serviceClass
    )
)
```

Attribute Definitions

The following are the new attribute types used in the Dynamic RADIUS Person class as defined by Aboba in his Internet draft:

```
( radius dynamicRadiusPersonClass 1
    NAME 'userName'
```

```
DESC 'the name of the user'
        EQUALITY caseIgnoreIA5Match
        SYNTAX 'IA5String{128}'
        SINGLE-VALUE
    )

        ( radius dynamicRadiusPersonClass 4
          NAME 'nasIPAddress'
          DESC 'IP address of the NAS'
          EQUALITY caseIgnoreIA5Match
          SYNTAX 'IA5String{128}'
          SINGLE-VALUE
    )

        ( radius dynamicRadiusPersonClass 5
          NAME 'nasPort'
          DESC 'Physical port number of the NAS
                Authenticating the user'
          EQUALITY integerMatch
          SYNTAX 'INTEGER'
          SINGLE-VALUE
    )

        ( radius dynamicRadiusPersonClass 8
          NAME 'framedIPAddress'
          DESC 'IP address to be assigned to the user
                in dotted decimal notation'
          EQUALITY caseIgnoreIA5Match
          SYNTAX 'IA5String{128}'
          SINGLE-VALUE
        )

        ( radius dynamicRadiusPersonClass 25
          NAME 'class'
          DESC 'The service class for the user'
          EQUALITY caseIgnoreIA5Match
          SYNTAX 'IA5String{128}'
        )

        ( radius dynamicRadiusPersonClass 30
          NAME 'calledStationId'
          DESC 'Phone number to which the user placed the
                call'
          EQUALITY caseIgnoreIA5Match
          SYNTAX 'IA5String{128}'
```

```
                                )

                        ( radius dynamicRadiusPersonClass 31
                            NAME 'callingStationId'
                            DESC 'Phone number from which the user placed
                                the call'
                            EQUALITY caseIgnoreIA5Match
                            SYNTAX 'IA5String{128}'
                        )

                        ( radius dynamicRadiusPersonClass 32

             NAME 'nasIdentifier'
                            DESC 'String identifying the NAS'
                            EQUALITY caseIgnoreIA5Match
                            SYNTAX 'IA5String{128}'
                            SINGLE-VALUE
                        )

                        ( radius dynamicRadiusPersonClass 42
                            NAME 'acctInputOctets'
                            DESC 'How many octets have been received from
                                the port during the session'
                            EQUALITY integerMatch
                            SYNTAX 'INTEGER'
                            SINGLE-VALUE
                        )

                        ( radius dynamicRadiusPersonClass 43
                            NAME 'acctOutputOctets'
                            DESC 'How many octets have been sent to the port
                                during the session'
                            EQUALITY integerMatch
                            SYNTAX 'INTEGER'
                            SINGLE-VALUE
                        )

                        ( radius dynamicRadiusPersonClass 44
                            NAME 'acctSessionId'
                            DESC 'Unique Accounting ID string for the
                                session'
                            EQUALITY caseIgnoreIA5Match
                            SYNTAX 'IA5String{128}'
                            SINGLE-VALUE
                        )
```

```
( radius dynamicRadiusPersonClass 45
    NAME 'acctAuthentic'
    DESC 'Indicates how the user was authenticated.
        Values include RADIUS
            (1), Local (2), Remote (3)'
    EQUALITY integerMatch
    SYNTAX 'INTEGER'
    SINGLE-VALUE
)

( radius dynamicRadiusPersonClass 46
    NAME 'acctSessionTime'
    DESC 'How many seconds the user has received
        service for'
    EQUALITY integerMatch
    SYNTAX 'INTEGER'
    SINGLE-VALUE
)

( radius dynamicRadiusPersonClass 47
    NAME 'acctInputPackets'
    DESC 'How many packets have been received from
        the port during the session'
    EQUALITY integerMatch
    SYNTAX 'INTEGER'
    SINGLE-VALUE
)

( radius dynamicRadiusPersonClass 48
    NAME 'acctOutputPackets'
    DESC 'How many packets have been sent to the
        port during the session'
    EQUALITY integerMatch
    SYNTAX 'INTEGER'
    SINGLE-VALUE
)

( radius dynamicRadiusPersonClass 49
    NAME 'acctTerminateCause'
    DESC 'Integer identifying how the session was
        terminated.'
    EQUALITY integerMatch
    SYNTAX 'INTEGER'
    SINGLE-VALUE
```

```
                                   )

                        ( radius dynamicRadiusPersonClass 50
                            NAME 'acctMultiSessionId'
                            DESC 'Unique string linking together multiple
                                related sessions.'
                            EQUALITY caseIgnoreIA5Match
                            SYNTAX 'IA5String{128}'
                        )

                        ( radius dynamicRadiusPersonClass 51
                            NAME 'acctLinkCount'
                            DESC 'Count of links in a multilink session at
                                time of last measurement.'
                            EQUALITY integerMatch
                            SYNTAX 'INTEGER'
                        )

                        ( radius dynamicRadiusPersonClass 52
                            NAME 'acctInputGigawords'
                            DESC 'This is an extended accounting attribute,
                                included to allow for keeping track of
                                long or fast sessions. If used, it
                                represents bits 32-63 of the number of
                                inbound octets during the session.'
                            EQUALITY integerMatch
                            SYNTAX 'INTEGER'
                            SINGLE-VALUE
                        )

                        ( radius dynamicRadiusPersonClass 53
                            NAME 'acctOutputGigawords'
                            DESC 'This is an extended accounting attribute,
                                included to allow for keeping track of
                                long or fast sessions. If used, it
                                represents bits 32-63 of the number of
                                outbound octets during the session.'
                            EQUALITY integerMatch
                            SYNTAX 'INTEGER'
                            SINGLE-VALUE
                        )
                  ( radius dynamicRadiusPersonClass 61
                            NAME 'nasPortType'
                            DESC 'Port on which the user has logged in.
                                Values include Async(1), Sync(2), ISDN
```

```
            Sync(3), V.120(4), V.110(5) and
            Virtual(6).'
       EQUALITY integerMatch
       SYNTAX 'INTEGER'
   )


( radius dynamicRadiusPersonClass 64
       NAME 'tunnelType'
       DESC 'Type of tunnel set up. Values include
             PPTP(1), L2F(2), L2TP(3), ATMP(4), VTP(5),
             AH(6), IP-IP(7)'
       EQUALITY integerMatch
       SYNTAX 'INTEGER'
       SINGLE-VALUE
   )


( radius dynamicRadiusPersonClass 65
       NAME 'tunnelMediumType'
       DESC 'Medium tunnel runs over. Values include
             IP(1), X.25(2), ATM(3), Frame Relay(4).'
       EQUALITY integerMatch
       SYNTAX 'INTEGER'
       SINGLE-VALUE
   )


( radius dynamicRadiusPersonClass 66
       NAME 'acctTunnelClientEndpoint'
       DESC 'This is the address of the Tunnel Client
             Endpoint.'
       EQUALITY caseIgnoreIA5Match
       SYNTAX 'IA5String{128}'
       SINGLE-VALUE
   )


( radius dynamicRadiusPersonClass 67
       NAME 'tunnelServerEndpoint'
       DESC 'The address of the tunnel server. The
             format of the string depends on the
             tunnelMediumType attribute.'
       EQUALITY integerMatch
       SYNTAX 'INTEGER'
       SINGLE-VALUE
   )


( radius dynamicRadiusPersonClass 68
```

```
                          NAME 'acctTunnelConnection'
                          DESC 'This is the connection Id assigned to the
                               call; it is included in Accounting-Request
                               packets and written to ILS. A tag field
                               lives in the first four octets.'
                          EQUALITY caseIgnoreIA5Match
                          SYNTAX 'IA5String{128}'
                          SINGLE-VALUE
                    )
          ( radius dynamicRadiusPersonClass 69
                          NAME 'tunnelPrivateGroupId'
                          DESC 'This is the private group Id assigned to
                               the call. A tag field lives in the first
                               four octets.'
                          EQUALITY caseIgnoreIA5Match
                          SYNTAX 'IA5String{128}'
                          SINGLE-VALUE
                    )

          ( radius dynamicRadiusPersonClass 77
                          NAME 'connectInfo'
                          DESC 'This is the connect string returned by
                               the modem in the initial connection, or by
                               post-termination diagnostics.'
                          EQUALITY caseIgnoreIA5Match
                          SYNTAX 'IA5String{128}'
                    )

          ( radius  dynamicRadiusPersonClass 257
                          NAME 'authenticationType'
                          DESC 'This attribute indicates the
                               authentication type for the user. Values
                               include PAP (1), CHAP(2), EAP(3),
                               MS-CHAP(4), and SPAP(5).'
                          EQUALITY integerMatch
                          SYNTAX 'INTEGER'
                          SINGLE-VALUE
                    )

          ( radius  dynamicRadiusPersonClass 258
                          NAME 'eapType'
                          DESC 'This attribute indicates the EAP type for
                               this user. It should only have a value when
                               EAP is enabled for the user.'
                          EQUALITY integerMatch
```

```
          SYNTAX 'INTEGER'
          SINGLE-VALUE
       )


   ( radius dynamicRadiusPersonClass 259
       NAME 'encryptionType'
       DESC 'Encryption type used (40-bit RC4 (1),
           128-bit RC4 (2)).'
       EQUALITY integerMatch
       SYNTAX 'INTEGER'
       SINGLE-VALUE
   )


   ( radius dynamicRadiusPersonClass 260
       NAME 'sessionLocalStartTime'
       DESC 'This is a timestamp giving session start
           in local time.'
       EQUALITY caseIgnoreIA5Match
       SYNTAX 'IA5String{128}'
       SINGLE-VALUE
   )


   ( radius dynamicRadiusPersonClass 261
NAME 'sessionLocalEndTime'
       DESC 'This is a timestamp giving session end in
           local time.'
       EQUALITY caseIgnoreIA5Match
       SYNTAX 'IA5String{128}'
       SINGLE-VALUE
   )


   ( radius dynamicRadiusPersonClass 262
       NAME 'ispId'
       DESC 'String identifying the local ISP to which
           the user is connected'
       EQUALITY caseIgnoreIA5Match
       SYNTAX 'IA5String{128}'
       SINGLE-VALUE
   )


   ( radius dynamicRadiusPersonClass 263
       NAME 'connectionStatus'
       DESC 'Indicates status of the connection. Values
           include Failed Authentication (1), Logged
           On (2), or Logged Off (3).'
```

```
                    EQUALITY integerMatch
                    SYNTAX 'INTEGER'
                    SINGLE-VALUE
                  )

                ( radius dynamicRadiusPersonClass 264
                    NAME 'serviceClass'
                    DESC ' String identifying class of service given
                        to user.'
                    EQUALITY caseIgnoreIA5Match
                    SYNTAX 'IA5String{128}'
                    SINGLE-VALUE
                  )
```

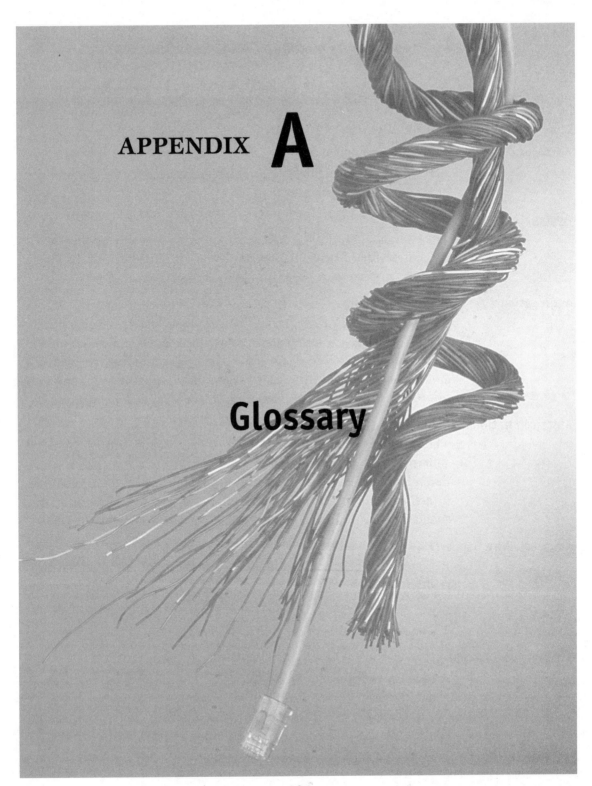

APPENDIX **A**

Glossary

Address

In the Internet, the exact network location of a computer or a node, addresses can be numerical or name; an IP identifier for an interface or set of interfaces.

Adjacency

A relationship formed between neighboring routers for the purpose of exchanging routing information.

Aggregate control

The control of multiple streams using a single timeline by the server; for audio/video feeds, this means that the client may issue a single play or pause message to control both audio and video feeds.

Aggregation

A strong form of an *association*. For example, the containment relationship between a system and the components that make up the system can be called an aggregation. An aggregation is expressed as a *qualifier* on the association class. Aggregation often implies, but does not require, that the aggregated *objects* have mutual dependencies.

American National Standards Institute (ANSI)

The principal standards development body in the United States; it consists of voluntary members that represent the U.S. in the International Standards Organization (ISO). Membership includes manufacturers, common carriers, and other national standards organizations, such as the Institute of Electrical and Electronic Engineers (IEEE).

American Wire Gauge (AWG)

A wire diameter specification; the lower the AWG number, the larger the wire diameter.

Amplitude

The maximum value of varying wave forms.

Anycast, anycast address

An identifier for a set of interfaces that typically belong to different nodes; a method developed for IPv6 of sending a datagram or packet to a single address with more than one interface. The packet is usually sent to the "nearest" node in a group of nodes, as determined by the routing protocols' measure of distance. Compare to *multicast* and *unicast*.

API

Application Programming Interface.

Application-Layer Gateway (ALG)

In modern usage, the term refers to systems that do translation from some native format to another; for example, a gateway that permits communication between TCP/IP systems and OSI systems. An application-layer gateway converts protocol data units (PDUs) from one stack's application protocol to the other stack's application protocol. Application-layer gateways act as origination and termination points for communications between realms.

Application Programming Interface (API)

A set of tools, routines, and protocols used as building blocks by programmers to develop programs; using APIs helps to keep applications consistent with the operating environment.

ASIC

Application-Specific Integrated Circuit.

Association

A *class* that expresses the relationship between two other classes; the relationship is established by the presence of two or more *references* in the association class pointing to the related classes.

Asymmetric Digital Subscriber Line (ADSL)

An xDSL technology in which modems attached to twisted-pair copper wires transmit from 1.5 to 8 Mbps downstream (to the subscriber) and from 16 to 640 Kbps upstream, depending on the line distance.

Asymmetric reachability

A link where non-reflexive and/or non-transitive reachability is part of normal operation; non-reflexive reachability means packets from A reach B but packets from B do not reach A. Non-transitive reachability means packets from A reach B, and packets from B reach C, but packets from A do not reach C. Many radio links exhibit these properties.

Asynchronous Transfer Mode (ATM)

A cell-switching and multiplexing technology that provides high-speed backbone support defined at 155 Mb/s and 622 Mb/s and having a 53-byte fixed-length cell consisting of a 5-byte header for routing information and 48 bytes of data.

Attachment Unit Interface (AUI)

A 15-pin shielded, twisted pair Ethernet cable that can be used to connect between network devices and an MAU.

Authentication

The process of knowing that the data received are the same as the data sent and that the sender is the actual sender; usually verified by a password; however, since passwords can be guessed or discovered, a system that requires an encrypted password and a key to decrypt it are becoming popular.

Autonomous system

A collection of CIDR IP address prefixes under common management; an autonomous system can be perceived as a set of routers under a single technical administration. An AS uses one or more interior gateway protocols and common metrics to route packets within the AS. It uses an exterior gateway protocol to route packets to other autonomous systems. The administration of an AS appears to other autonomous systems to have a single coherent interior routing plan and presents a consistent picture of what networks are reachable through it.

Backbone network

The major transmission path for network interconnection.

Bandwidth

The signaling rate of a LAN or WAN circuit or the number of bits or bytes that can be transmitted over the channel each second and measured by electrical engineers in Hertz (Hz). See also *latency*.

BER

Basic Encoding Rules.

BNC Connector

Bayonet Neill-Concelman connector; a type of connector used for attaching coaxial cable to electronic equipment that can be attached or detached more quickly than connectors that screw. ThinWire Ethernet (IEEE 802.3 10BASE2) uses BNC connectors.

BOOTP

The Bootstrap Protocol; a transport mechanism for the collection of configuration information. BOOTP is widely deployed throughout the TCP/IP community, particularly in diskless workstations.

BOOTP relay agent

an Internet host or router that passes DHCP messages between DHCP clients and DHCP servers. See *relay agent*.

Broadband

A data transmission technique allowing multiple high-speed signals to share the bandwidth of a single cable via frequency division multiplexing.

Broadcast

A type of data communication in which a source sends one copy of a message to all the nodes on the network even if the node does not want to receive such messages. See also *anycast, unicast, multicast,* and *IP multicasting*.

Broadcast domain

The part of a network that receives the same broadcasts.

Broadcast network

A network that supports more than two attached routers and has the capability to address a single physical message to all the attached routers.

Building backbone subsystem

Provides the link between the building and campus backbone.

Campus backbone subsystem

Provides the link between buildings and contains the cabling and crossconnects between clusters of buildings within a site.

Cardinality

A relationship between two classes that allows more than one object to be related to a single object. For example, Microsoft Office is made up of the software elements Word, Excel, Access and PowerPoint.

Carrier Sense Multiple Access with Collision Detection (CSMA/CD)

The channel access method used by the Ethernet and ISO 8802-3 LANs. Each station waits for an idle channel before transmitting and detects overlapping transmissions by other stations.

Carrierless Amplitude Phase (CAP) modulation

A version of Quadrature Amplitude Modulation (QAM) that stores parts of a modulated message signal in memory and then reassembles the parts in the modulated wave; the carrier signal is suppressed before transmission because it contains no information and is reassembled at the receiving modem (hence the word "carrierless" in CAP).

CBC

Cipher-Block Chaining.

Central Office (CO)

A facility that contains the lowest node in the hierarchy of switches that comprise the public telephone network.

Channel

The data path between two nodes.

CIM

Common Information Model is the schema of the overall managed environment. It is divided into a core model, common model and extended schemas.

CIM schema

The schema representing the core and common models. Versions of this schema will be released by the DMTF over time as the schema evolves.

Class

A collection of instances, all of which support a common type; that is, a set of *properties* and *methods*. The common properties and methods are defined as *features* of the class. For example, the class called Modem represents all the modems present in a system.

Class A IP address

A type of unicast IP address that segments the address space into many network addresses and few host addresses.

Class B IP address

A type of unicast IP address that segments the address space into a medium number of network and host addresses.

Class C IP address

A type of unicast IP address that segments the address space into many host addresses and few network addresses.

Class D IP addresses

Specifies multicast host groups in IPv4-based networks; the Internet standard in "dotted decimal" notation assigns this host group addresses range from 224.0.0.0 to 239.255.255.255.

Classless Inter-Domain Routing Protocol (CIDR)

CIDR is an IP addressing scheme that replaces the older system based on classes A, B, and C. With CIDR, a single IP address can be used to designate many unique IP addresses. A CIDR IP address looks like a normal IP address except that it ends with a slash followed by a number, called the IP prefix. For example: 172.200.0.0/16

Client

The client requests continuous media data from the media server.

Client/server architecture

A network architecture in which the protocols in use govern the behavior of workstations so each one works either as a client or a server; users run applications on client machines while server machines manage network resources.

CLNP

OSI Connectionless Network Protocol.

Common model

A collection of models specific to a particular area, derived from the core model. Included are the *system model*, the *application model*, the *network model*, and the *device model*.

Conference

A multiparty, multimedia presentation, where "multi" implies greater than or equal to one.

Confidentiality

The process of communicating in such a way that only the recipient can determine and knows what has been sent.

Connection

A transport-layer virtual circuit established between two programs for the purpose of communication.

Connectionless protocol

A type of network protocol in which a host can send a message without establishing a connection with the recipient; the host puts the message onto the network, provides the destination address and hopes that the message arrives at its destination.

Connection-oriented protocol

A protocol that requires the establishment of a channel between the sender and receiver before transmitting any data; the telephone, TCP, and HTTP are all examples of connection-oriented protocols.

Consumer

Defined in the Multicast Transport Protocol as a transport capable only of receiving user data; it can transmit control packets, such as negative acknowledgments, but can never transmit any requests for the transmit token or any form of data or empty messages.

Container file

A file that may contain multiple media streams, which often comprise a presentation when played together; RTSP servers may offer aggregate control on these files, though the concept of a container file is not embedded in the protocol.

Continuous media

Data where a timing relationship exists between source and sink; that is, the sink must reproduce the timing relationship that existed at the source. The most common examples of continuous media are audio and motion video. Continuous media can be real-time (interactive), where there is a "tight" timing relationship between source and sink, or streaming (playback), where the relationship is less strict.

Convergence

The amount of time it takes for a change to a routing topology to propagate throughout the network.

COPS

Common Open Policy Service.

Core Based Trees (CBT) routing protocol

The CBT routing protocol is characterized by a single tree shared by all members of the group, who receive multicast traffic over this shared tree regardless of the source of the message. A small number of core routers constructs the tree and routers can join the tree by sending a join message to the core.

Core model

A subset of CIM, not specific to any platform; the core model is set of classes and associations that establish a conceptual framework for the schema of the rest of the managed environment. Systems, applications, networks and related information are modeled as extensions to the core model.

Core network

A combination of switching offices and transmission plant that connects switching offices; in the U.S. local exchange, core networks are linked by several competing interexchange networks. In the rest of the world, core networks extend to national boundaries.

CoS

Class of Service.

Counter-rotating Ring

A method of using two ring networks going in opposite directions (such as in FDDI) to provide redundancy; the network interfaces can change the path of the ring the data flow around. This preserves the ring and the operation of the LAN even if some of the cable is unplugged or cut, or if a device on the ring fails in such a way that it cannot transmit data around the ring.

CPE

Customer Premises Equipment.

DAP

Directory Access Protocol.

Data Circuit Terminating Equipment (DCE)

An interface typically found in modems or similar devices that provide clocking as well as switching services between DTE.

Data Link Connection Identifier (DLCI)

A 10-bit value included in the address field of a frame relay packet that uniquely identifies each virtual circuit at each frame relay.

Data Terminal Equipment (DTE)

An interface typically embodied in computers, terminals, or routers that act as terminating equipment for a given network.

Datagram

Term used in IPv4; the format for a packet of data sent on the Internet to a specific destination address; specifies standards for the header information; in IPv6, datagrams are known as packets.

Datagram-based protocol

A type of protocol that imposes a maximum size on the amount of data that can be sent at one time; this type of protocol is analogous to sending a postcard through the postal service to a friend. The size of the card limits the amount of data that can be sent.

DBMS

Database Management System.

DEN

Directory-Enabled Networks.

Dense-mode multicast routing protocols

A category of routing protocol that assumes that multicast group members are densely distributed throughout the network; the basic assumption is that almost all the hosts on the network belong to the group. Dense-mode routing protocols include the Distance Vector Multicast Routing Protocol (DVMRP), Multicast Open Shortest Path First (MOSPF), and Protocol-Independent Multicast - Dense Mode (PIM-DM) protocols. See also sparse-mode routing protocols.

DHCP (Dynamic Host Configuration Protocol)

DHCP is an extension of BOOTP that adds the capability of automatic allocation of reusable addresses and configuration information. See RFC 1541.

Dialup

A type of communication established by a switched circuit connection using the public telephone network.

DIB

Directory Information Base.

Digital Loop Carrier (DLC)

The carrier's local loop infrastructure that connects end-users located more than 18,000 feet or 3.5 miles away from the central office;

DLC systems consist of physical pedestals containing line cards that concentrate residential links onto digital circuits.

Digital Subscriber Line (DSL)

A local loop access technology that calls for modems on either end of copper twisted-pair wire to deliver data, voice, and video information over a dedicated digital network.

Digital Subscriber Line Access Multiplexer (DSLAM)

Multiplexing equipment that contains a high concentration of central office splitters, xDSL modems, and other electronics to connect traffic to the WAN.

Discrete Multi-Tone (DMT) modulation

A wave modulation scheme that discretely divides the available frequencies into 256 subchannels or tones to avoid high-frequency signal loss caused by noise on copper lines.

Discrete Wavelet Multi-Tone (DWMT)

A variant of DMT modulation; DWMT goes a step further in complexity and performance by creating even more isolation between sub-channels.

DISP

Directory Information Shadowing Protocol.

Distance Vector Multicast Routing Protocol (DVMRP)

The first protocol developed to support multicast routing and used widely on the Mbone; RFC 1075 describes this. DVMRP assume that every host on the network belongs to the multicast group.

DIT

Directory Information Tree.

DMI

Desktop Management Interface.

DMTF

Desktop Management Task Force.

DN

Distinguished Name.

DNS

Domain Name Service.

Domain

A virtual room for object names that establishes the range in which the names of objects are unique.

Domain

Resources under control of a single administration.

Domain name

The name assigned to a grouping of computers (the domain) for administrative purposes; domain names are usually assigned to a company.

Domain Name Service (DNS)

The name service of the TCP/IP protocol family; it provides information about computers on local and remote networks. DNS is an Internet-wide hierarchical database.

Domain of Interpretation (DOI)

A DOI defines payload formats, exchange types, and conventions for naming security-relevant information such as security policies or cryptographic algorithms and modes.

DPP

Distributed Packet Pipelining.

DSA

Directory System Agent.

DSP

Directory Service Protocol.

DTE/DCE

The interface between Data Terminal Equipment (DTE) and Data Circuit-terminating Equipment (DCE); one of the most common in networking.

DUA

Directory User Agent.

E1

The European basic multiplex rate that carries 30 voice channels in a 256-bit frame transmitted at 2.048 Mbps.

Echo cancellation

A technique used by ADSL, V.32, and V.34 modems that isolates and filters unwanted signal energy from echoes caused by the main transmitted signal.

Encryption

Conversion of human-readable data (plain text) into encoded data (cipher text) that can be decoded only with a specific key.

Entity

The information transferred as the payload of a request or response. An entity consists of meta-information in the form of entity-header fields and content in the form of an entity.

ESP

See *IP Encapsulating Security Payload*.

European Telecom Standards Institute (ETSI)

A consortium of manufacturers, service carriers, and others responsible for setting technical standards in the European telecommunications industry.

Explicit qualifier

A qualifier defined separately from the definition of a class, property or other schema element (see *implicit qualifier*). Explicit qualifier names must be unique across the entire schema. Implicit qualifier names must be unique within the defining schema element; that is, a given schema element may not have two qualifiers with the same name.

Extended schema

A platform specific schema derived from the common model. An example is the Win32 schema.

Fanout

The degree of replication in a multicast tree or the number of copies of a call in a switch; associated with IP multicasting and ATM.

Fast Ethernet

A nickname for the 100Mbps version of IEEE 802.3.

Fast packet

A data transmission technique in which the packet is transmitted without any error checking along the route. The endpoints have the responsibility of performing any error checking.

Feature

A *property* or *method* belonging to a class.

Fiber Distributed Data Interface (FDDI)

A set of ANSI/ISO standards to define a high-bandwidth (100 Mbps) general-purpose LAN; FDDI primarily runs over optical fiber but can also run over copper. FDDI provides synchronous and asynchronous services between computers and peripheral equipment in a time-token passing dual-ring configuration.

FIRE

Flexible Intelligent Routing Engine.

Flat network

A group of machines on a LAN logically partitioned by the use of Ethernet or token ring switches into a virtual network (VLAN) to reduce LAN network congestion; the switch does not partition the network to different subnets.

Flavor

Part of a qualifier specification indicating overriding and *inheritance* rules. For example, the qualifier KEY has Flavor (DisableOverride ToSubclass), meaning that every subclass must inherit it and cannot override it.

Flooding

The part of the OSPF protocol that distributes and synchronizes the link-state database between OSPF routers.

Flow-based

A proprietary implementation of Layer 3 switching that investigates only the first packet of data, switching the remaining packets at Layer 2.

Fragment

A portion of a packet/frame and often a part of an Ethernet frame left over from a collision; in IP terminology, fragment means a packet that is the result of splitting a larger packet into smaller ones.

Frame

In telecommunications, a unit of data transmitted between network points complete with addressing and necessary protocol control information.

Frame relay network

A network consisting of frame relay switches, offering a bare-bones link-layer service for fast bulk packet transmission.

Frequency

The rate of signal oscillation in hertz (Hz).

Frequency Division Multiplexing (FDM)

A technique that divides the available bandwidth of a channel into a number of separate channels.

FTP

File Transfer Protocol.

Full duplex

The property of a data-communications line that provides independent, simultaneous two-way transmission in both directions, as opposed to half-duplex transmission; the alternatives are *half duplex* and *simplex*.

Gateway

An intermediate destination by which packets are delivered to their ultimate destination; a host address of another router directly reachable through an attached network. As with any host address it can be specified symbolically.

Gigabit Ethernet

High-speed version of Ethernet (a billion bits per second) under development by the IEEE.

Half duplex

A possible property of a data-communications line: that data can be transferred in either direction, but only in one direction at a time; if the line is sufficiently high speed, then to a human it may appear that data transfer is simultaneous in both directions if the two ends quickly take turns transferring. The alternatives are *full duplex* and *simplex*.

Heartbeat

An interval of time nominally measured in milliseconds; a key parameter in the transport's state. It can be adapted to the requirements of the transport's client to provide the desired quality of service; also an Ethernet-defined SQE signal quality test function.

Hertz

A frequency unit equal to one cycle per second.

High bit rate Digital Subscriber Line (HDSL)

An xDSL technology in which modems on either end of two or more twisted-pair lines deliver symmetric T1 or E1 speeds; currently, T1 requires two lines and E1 requires three.

High-Definition Television (HDTV)

A system of transmitting television signals at 24 Mbps; this increases the horizontal lines of resolution from 480 to 560 lines per display.

Host Group

All hosts belonging to a multicast session; the membership of a host group is dynamic: hosts can join and leave the group at any time. There can be any number of members in a host group and the members can be located anywhere on the local network or on the Internet. A host can be a member of more than one group at a time.

Host, host computer

Any node that is not a router; any end-user computer, such as a personal computer or workstation that is part of a local area network, or any other system that connects to a network and functions as the endpoint of a data transfer on the Internet.

Host-oriented keying

A keying method in which all users on host 1 share the same key for use on traffic destined for all users on host 2

HTTP

Hypertext Transfer Protocol.

ICMP

Internet Message Control Protocol for IPv6; the terms ICMPv4 and ICMPv6 are used only in contexts where it is necessary to avoid ambiguity.

ICMP destination unreachable indication

An error indication returned to the original sender of a packet that cannot be delivered for the reasons outlined in ICMP; if the error occurs on a node other than the node originating the packet, an ICMP error message is generated. If the error occurs on the originating node, an implementation is not required to create and send an ICMP error packet to the source, as long as the upper-layer sender is notified through an appropriate mechanism; for example, the return value from a procedure call. Note, however, that an implementation may find it convenient in some cases to return errors to the sender by taking the offending packet, generating an ICMP error message, and then delivering it locally through the generic error handling routines.

IEEE

Institute of Electrical and Electronic Engineers.

IETF

Internet Engineering Task Force.

Implicit Qualifier

A qualifier defined as a part of the definition of a class, property or other schema element (see *explicit qualifier*).

Indication

A type of class usually created as a result of the occurrence of a *trigger*.

Inheritance

A relationship between two classes in which all the members of the *subclass* are required to be members of the *superclass*. Any member of the subclass must also support any method or property supported by the superclass. For example, modem is a subclass of device.

Instance

A unit of data. An instance is a set of *property* values that can be uniquely identified by a *key*.

Integrated Services Digital Network (ISDN)

All digital service provided by telephone companies; provides 144 Kbps over a single phone line (divided in two 64 Kbps "B" channels and one 16 Kbps "D" channel).

Integrity

Ensuring that data are transmitted from a source to a destination without alteration.

Interexchange Carrier (IEC)

A long-distance service provider.

Interface

A system's attachment point to a link; it is possible for a system to have more than one interface to the same link. Interfaces are uniquely identified by IP unicast addresses; a single interface may have more than one such address. An interface can be a connection between a router and one of its attached networks. A single IP address, domain name, or interface name can specify a physical interface (unless the network is an unnumbered point-to-point network).

Internet

The connection of the uncountable, dissimilar networks of computers throughout the world using TCP/IP to exchange data; differentiate this from internet, with a lowercase i, which is a local network that shares a common communications protocol.

Internet Assigned Numbers Authority (IANA)

The central coordinator for the assignment of unique parameter values for Internet protocols; the IANA is chartered by the Internet Society (ISOC) and the Federal Network Council (FNC) to act as the clearing house to assign and coordinate the use of Internet protocol parameters.

Internet datagram

The unit of data exchanged between an Internet module and the higher-level protocol together with the Internet header.

Internet Engineering Task Force (IETF)

An international group of network designers, operators, vendors, and researchers, closely aligned to the Internet Architecture Board and chartered to work on the design and engineering of TCP/IP and the global Internet; the IETF is divided into groups or areas, each with a manager and is open to any interested individual.

Internet Group Management Protocol (IGMP)

Multicast routers use this protocol to learn the existence of host group members on their directly attached subnets. IP hosts use IGMP to report their host group memberships to any immediately neighboring multicast routers. IGMP messages are encapsulated in IP datagrams, with an IP protocol number of 2. RFC1112 describes

IGMP, which is considered an extension to ICMP and occupies the same place in the IP protocol stack.

Internet Protocol (IP)

The protocol or standard at the network level of the Internet that defines the packets of information, their routing to remote nodes, the method of addressing remote computers, and routing packets to remote hosts.

Internet Service Provider (ISP)

Businesses that provide subscription services, such as online information retrieval software, bulletin boards, electronic mail, and so on, to users for a fee; domains under the control of a single administration that share their resources with other domains.

Internetwork Packet Exchange protocol (IPX)

A datagram protocol found in Novell NetWare networks; similar to UDP and together with SPX, provides connectionless services similar to UDP/IP.

InterNIC

A collaborative project between AT&T and Network Solutions, Inc. (NSI) supported by the National Science Foundation; the project currently offers the following four services to users of the Internet.

IP Encapsulating Security Payload (ESP)

A mechanism that seeks to provide confidentiality and integrity by encrypting data to be protected and placing the encrypted data in the data portion of the ESP.

IP multicast

A one-to-many transmission described in RFC 1112; the transmission of an IP datagram to a "host group", a set of zero or more hosts identified by a single IP destination address. A multicast datagram is delivered to all members of its destination host group with the same "best-efforts" reliability as regular unicast IP datagrams.

IP multicast datagram

A datagram delivered to all members of the multicast host group; delivered with the same best-effort reliability as are regular unicast IP datagrams.

IP multicast router

A router supporting IGMP and one or more of the multicast routing protocols, including Distance DVMRP, MOSPF, PIM-DM, CBT, and PIM-SM.

IPSO (IP Security Option)

U.S. Department of Defense protocol for protecting datagrams over the network and defined in RFC 1108.

IPX

See *Internetwork Packet Exchange protocol*.

ISE

Intelligent Switching Engine.

ISO (International Standards Organization)

A special agency of the United Nations charged with the development of communication standards for computers; membership in the ISO consists of representatives from international standards organizations throughout the world.

ISO

International Standards Organization.

ISP

Internet Service Provider.

ITU

International Telecommunication Union.

ITU-T

International Telecommunication Union-Telecommunication Standardization Sector.

Kbps

Kilobits per second.

Key

One or more qualified class properties that can be used to construct a name.

LAN

A local area network; a communication network that spans a limited geographical area. LANs can differ from one another by topology or arrangement of devices on the network, the protocols they use, and the media, such as twisted-pair wire, coaxial cables, or fiber optic cables, used to connect the devices on the network.

Latency

The transmission delay of the network or the minimum amount of time it takes for any one of those bits or bytes to travel across the network. See also *bandwidth*.

LDAP

Lightweight Directory Access Protocol.

LDP

Local Decision Point.

LEO system

A low-earth-orbit satellite system consisting of a number of small satellites orbiting in a circular orbit at over, or nearly over, the geographic poles and flying at an altitude of a few hundred miles; wireless access to the Internet is dependent upon this type of satellite.

LLC

Logical Link Control.

Local loop

The line from a subscriber to the telephone company central office.

Logical link

A temporary connection between source and destination nodes, or between two processes on the same node.

Logical Link Control (LLC)

Part of the data link layer of the OSI model and the link-layer control specification for the IEEE 802.x series of standards; it defines the services for the transmission of data between two stations with no intermediate switching stations. There are three versions: LLC1 is connectionless, LLC2 is connection oriented, and LLC3 is connectionless with acknowledgment.

Logical topologies

Describe the view of the network as seen by the network's components access methods or rules of operation.

MAC address

The unique media access control 6-byte address that is associated with the network adapter card and uniquely identifies the machine on a particular network; a MAC address is also known as an Ethernet address, hardware address, station address, or physical address.

Managed object

The actual item in the system environment that is accessed by the *provider*: for example, a Network Interface Card.

Mask

A means of subdividing networks using address modification; a mask is a dotted quad specifying which bits of the destination are significant. Except when used in a route filter, GateD only supports contiguous masks.

Maximum Transmission Units (MTU)

The largest amount of data that can be transferred across a network; size is determined by the network hardware.

Mbone

A virtual multicast backbone network layered on top of the physical Internet; in existence for about five years, the Mbone supports routing of IP Multicast packets.

Mbps

Abbreviation for megabits per second.

Media initialization

Data type/codec specific initialization; this includes such things as clock rates, color tables, etc. Any transport-independent information, required by a client for playback of a media stream occurs in the media initialization phase of stream setup.

Media parameter

Parameter specific to a media type that may be changed before or during stream playback.

Media server

The server providing playback or recording services for one or more media streams; different media streams within a presentation may originate from different media servers. A media server may reside on the same or a different host as the Web server the presentation is invoked from.

Media server indirection

Redirection of a media client to a different media server.

Media stream

A single media instance, such as an audio stream or a video stream as well as a single whiteboard or shared application group; in RTP, a stream consists of all RTP and RTCP packets created by a source within an RTP session. This is equivalent to the definition of a DSM-CC stream.

Medium Attachment Unit (MAU)

A device used to convert signals from one Ethernet medium to another.

Meta-model

A set of classes, associations and properties that expresses the types of things that can be defined in a Schema. For example, the meta-model includes a class called property which defines the properties known to the system, a class called method which defines the methods known to the system, and a class called class which defines the classes known to the system.

Meta-schema

The schema of the meta-model.

Method

A declaration of a signature; that is, the method name, return type and parameters; in the case of a concrete class this may imply an implementation.

MIB

Management Information Base.

Midband

A communication channel with a bandwidth range of 28.8 to 56 Kbps.

MIF

Management Information Format.

Model

A set of classes, properties and associations that allows the expression of information about a specific domain. For example, a network may consist of network devices and logical networks. The network devices may have attachment associations to each other, and may have member associations to logical networks.

Model Path

A reference to an object within a namespace.

Modem

Contraction for modulator/demodulator. A modem converts the serial digital data from a transmitting device into a form suitable for transmission over the analog telephone channel.

Modulation

The process in which the characteristics of one wave or signal are varied in accordance with another wave or signal. Modulation can alter frequency, phase, or amplitude characteristics.

Multiaccess network

A physical network that supports the attachment of more than two routers; each pair of routers on such a network can communicate directly.

Multicast

Method of transmitting messages from a host using a singe transmission to a selected subset of all the hosts that can receive the messages; also a message that is sent out to multiple devices on the network by a host. See also *anycast, unicast, broadcast*, and *IP multicasting*.

Multicast group

A group set up to receive messages from a source; these groups can be set up based on frame relay or IP in the TCP/IP protocol suite, as well as in other networks.

Multicast interface

An interface to a to a link over which IP multicast or IP broadcast service is supported.

Multicast link

A link over which IP multicast or IP broadcast service is supported; this includes broadcast media such as LANs and satellite channels, single point-to-point links, and some store-and-forward networks such as SMDS networks.

Multicast Open Shortest Path First (MOSPF)

RFC 1584 defines MOSPF as an extension to the OSPF link-state unicast routing protocol that provides the ability to route IP multi-cast traffic. Some portions of the Mbone support MOSPF. MOSPF uses the OSPF link-state metric to determine the least-cost path and calculates a spanning tree for routing multicast traffic with the multi-cast source at the root and the group members as leaves.

Multicast Transport Protocol (MTP)

This protocol gives application programs guarantees of reliability. The MTP protocol could be useful when developing some types of applica-tions, such as distributed databases that need to be certain that all mem-bers of a multicast group agree on which packets have been received.

Multimode Fiber

A type of fiber mostly used for short distances such as those found in a campus LAN; it can carry 100 megabits/second for typical cam-pus distances, the actual maximum speed (given the right electron-ics) depending upon the actual distance. It is easier to connect to than single-mode fiber, but its limit on speed x distance is lower.

Multiplex

Combining signals of multiple channels into one channel; this process provides multiple users with access to a single conductor or medium by transmitting in multiple distinct frequency bands (fre-quency division multiplexing, or FDM) or by assigning the same channel to different users at different times (time division multiplex-ing, or TDM).

Multiplexer

A device that allows several users to share a single circuit and fun-nels different data streams into a single stream; at the other end of the communications link, another multiplexer reverses the process by splitting the data stream back into the original streams.

Multiplexing

A repeater, either standalone or connected to standard Ethernet cable, for interconnecting up to eight thin-wire Ethernet segments.

Name

Combination of a name space path and a model path that identifies a unique object.

Namespace

An object that defines a scope within which object keys must be unique.

Namespath Path

A reference to a name space within an implementation that is capable of hosting CIM objects.

NAP (Network Access Point)

a Internet hub where national and international ISPs connect with one another; a NAP router has to know about every network on the Internet.

Narrowband

A communication channel with a bandwidth of less than 28.8 Kbps.

NDS

NetWare Directory Services.

Neighboring

Having an IP address belonging to the same subnet.

NetBEUI

A enhanced version of the NetBIOS protocol and used by Windows based operating systems such as Windows 95 and Windows NT.

NetBIOS (Network Basic Input Output System)

An API with special functions for local area networks; used with the DOS BIOS.

Network Access Point (NAP)

An Internet hub where national and international ISPs connect with one another; a NAP router has to know about every network on the Internet.

Network address

The network address, or the node address of the machine where a service is available. See *IP address* and *network service access point (NSAP)*.

Network Information Center (NIC)

Central organization of a network with the authority to create network names and addresses; NIC.DDN.MIL is the specific Internet NIC that holds the authority to create root servers.

Network Information Service

Referred to as NIS and formerly known as Sun Yellow Pages, NIS is used for the administration of network-wide databases. NIS has two services, one for finding a NIS server, the other for access to the NIS databases. NIS permits dynamic updates of the database files. NIS is a non-hierarchical, replicated database which is the property of Sun Microsystems.

Node

Any intelligent device connected to the network; this includes terminal servers, host computers, and any other devices (such as printers and terminals) directly connected to the network. A node can be thought of as any device with a hardware address.

NOS

Network Operating System.

NTP

Network Time Protocol.

Open System Interconnection (OSI)

The name adopted by the International Organization for Standardization for its set of layered standards for computer communications; the aim of the standards is to permit communication-based services between computer systems of different vendors.

OSPF

Open Shortest Path First.

Packet

A package of data with a header which may or may not be logically complete; more often a physical packaging than a logical packaging of data; in IPv6, the name for datagram; the units of data a transmission is broken into so it can be sent in the most efficient and speedy manner across the network.

Packet-by-packet

An implementation of Layer 3 switching that uses industry-wide, standard routing protocols to examine all packets and forward them to their destination entirely in Layer 3.

Participant

Member of a conference; a participant may be a machine such as a media record or playback server.

Path MTU

Path Maximum Transmission Unit discovery; a method of determining the largest packet that can be sent between a source and destination. It is basically a modification to the IP, TCP, and UDP layers to accommodate the protocol. See RFC 1191.

PBX

Private Branch Exchange.

PDP

Policy Decision Point.

Peer-to-peer architecture

The arrangement of communication functions and services in layers so that data transmission between logical groups or layers in a network architecture occurs between entities in the same layer of the model; with a peer-to-peer architecture, all workstations in this type of network have the equivalent capabilities. See also *client/server architecture*.

PEP

Policy Enforcement Point.

Permanent Virtual Circuit (PVCP)

A permanent logical connection set up with packet data networks such as frame relay.

Phase modulation

A technique that changes the characteristics of a generated sine wave or signal so that it will carry information.

Physical layer

The physical channel implements Layer 1, the bottom layer of the OSI model. The physical layer insulates Layer 2 (the data-link layer) from medium-dependent physical characteristics such as baseband, broadband or fiberoptic transmission. Layer 1 defines the protocols that govern transmission media and signals.

Physical topologies

Define the arrangement of devices and the layout of the wiring.

PIM-Dense Mode (PIM-DM) Routing Protocol

Protocol-Independent Multicast Dense Mode is a protocol operates in an environment where group members are relatively densely packed. PIM-DM is similar to DVMRP in that it employs the Reverse Path Multicasting (RPM) algorithm. PIM-DM controls message processing, and data packet forwarding is integrated with PIM-SM operation so that a single router can run different modes for different groups.

Point-to-point networks

A network joining a single pair of routers; for example, a 56Kb serial line network.

Point-to-Point Protocol (PPP)

The successor to SLIP, PPP provides router-to-router and host-to-network connections over both synchronous and asynchronous circuits.

Polymorphism

A subclass may redefine the implementation of a method or property inherited from its superclass. The property or method is thereby redefined, even if the superclass is used to access the object. For example, device may define availability as a string, and may return the values "powersave", "on" or "off." The Modem subclass of device may redefine (override) availability by returning "on," "off," but not "powersave". If all devices are enumerated, any device that happens to be a modem will not return the value "powersave" for the availability property.

POP3 (Post Office Protocol, Version 3)

POP3 allows client systems to read the messages in a user's in box. It is typically used by PC clients to access a mail server. See RFC 1939.

Port number

A 16-bit number that ranges from zero to about 65,000 and is used for unique identification of services within a computer. Most computers on the Internet use well-known port numbers for the same server; for example, port 25 is reserved for SMTP-speaking mail and port 23 is reserved for Telnet-speaking communications. Privileged ports are those with port numbers below 1024 and in UNIX only *root* can start the servers that listen to them. Well-known ports fall within the range of zero through 255.

Port

The portion of a socket that specifies which logical input or output channel of a process is associated with the data.

POTS

Plain Old Telephone Service.

POTS splitter

A passive filter that separates voice traffic from data traffic.

Presentation

A set of one or more streams presented to the client as a complete media feed, using a presentation description; in most cases in the RTSP context, this implies aggregate control of those streams, but does not have to.

Presentation description

A presentation description contains information about one or more media streams within a presentation, such as the set of encodings, network addresses and information about the content.

Property

A value used to characterize an instance of a class; for example, a device may have a property called status.

Protocol

The set of rules to send and receive data and to govern activities within a specific layer of the network architecture model; protocols regulate the transfer of data between layers and across links to other devices and define procedures for handling lost or damaged transmissions or packets. The protocols also determine whether the network uses peer-to-peer or client/server architecture.

Proxy

A router that responds to neighbor discovery query messages on behalf of another node.

Public Switched Telephone Network (PSTN)
> A telephone system through which users can be connected by dialing specific telephone numbers.

Push
> A control bit that does not occupy a sequence space and indicates that this segment contains data that must be pushed through to the receiving user.

QoS
> Quality of Service

Quadrature Amplitude Modulation (QAM)
> A bandwidth conservation process routinely used in modems, QAM enables two digital carrier signals to occupy the same transmission bandwidth.

Qualifier
> A value used to characterize a method, property, or class in the meta-schema; if a property has the qualifier KEY with the value TRUE, the property is a key for the class.

RADIUS
> Remote Authorization Dial-In User Service.

Random delay
> The random amount of time a transmission is delayed to prevent multiple nodes from transmitting at exactly the same time, or to prevent long-range periodic transmissions from synchronizing with each other.

RAP
> RSVP Admission Policy.

Rate-Adaptive Digital Subscriber Line (R-ADSL)
> An emerging variation of CAP; it divides the transmission spectrum into discrete subchannels and adjusts each signal transmission according to line quality.

Reachability
> Whether or not the one-way forward path to a neighbor is functioning properly; for neighboring routers, reachability means that packets sent by a node's IP layer are delivered to the router's IP layer, and

the router is indeed forwarding packets. This means the node is configured as a router, not a host. For hosts, reachability means that packets sent by a node's IP layer are delivered to the neighbor host's IP layer.

Real-Time Streaming Protocol (RTSP)

This application-level protocol provides control for the delivery of data with real-time properties. RTSP enables controlled on-demand delivery of real-time data, such as audio and video.

RED

Random Early Detection.

Reference

Special property types that are references or "pointers" to other instances.

Regional Bell Operating Company (RBOC)

A telecommunication company formed as a result of the divestiture of AT&T; RBOCs oversee Bell operating companies.

Relay

A device that interconnects LANs, different kinds of relays include repeaters, bridges, routers, and gateways.

Relay agent

An Internet host or router that passes DHCP messages between DHCP clients and DHCP servers. DHCP messages have the same format as BOOTP messages. DHCP uses the same relay agent behavior specified in the BOOTP protocol. DHCP/BOOTP relay agents pass the message on to DHCP servers not on the same subnet.

Reliable multicast protocols

Reliable multicast protocols provide for reliable transmission of datagrams from a single source host to members of a multicast group. An example of a reliable multicast protocol is the Multicast Transport Protocol (MTP). This protocol gives application programs guarantees of reliability. See also *Multicast Transport Protocol (MTP)*.

Request for Comment (RFC)

An official document used by the IETF to create standards for use in the Internet.

Response

An RTSP response. If an HTTP response is meant, that is indicated explicitly.

Retention

Defined in the MTP as one of the three fundamental parameters that make up the transport's state (along with heartbeat and window); retention is a number of heartbeats, and though applied in several different circumstances, is primarily used as the number of heartbeats a producing client must maintain buffered data should it need to be retransmitted.

Reverse Address Resolution Protocol (RARP)

An Internet protocol that can be used by diskless hosts to find their Internet address. See RFC 903.

RIP (Routing Information Protocol)

An early BSD UNIX routing protocol that has become an industry standard.

RISC

Reduced Instruction Set Computing.

RMON

Remote Monitoring.

Route aggregation

A CIDR addressing in which a single high-level route entry can represent many lower-level routes in the global routing tables. The CIDR addressing scheme has a hierarchical structure.

Router

An internet device that connects two networks, either LANs or WANs, that use identical protocols; passes, or routes, data being sent between the two networks; a node that forwards IP packets not explicitly addressed to itself. *Also* a device that connects two networks at the network layer (Layer 3) of the OSI model; operated like a bridge but also can choose routes through a network.

Router ID

An IP address used as unique identifier assigned to represent a specific router. This is usually the address of an attached interface; also a 32-bit number assigned to each router running the OSPF protocol. This number uniquely identifies the router within the autonomous system.

Routing

In networking, the process of moving a packet of data from source to destination; routing is usually performed by a dedicated device called a router. Routing, a key feature of the Internet, enables messages to pass from one computer to another and eventually reach the target machine. Each intermediary computer performs routing by passing along the message to the next computer. Part of this process involves analyzing a routing table to determine the best path.

Routing table

A table of information on each machine that stores information about possible destination addresses and how to reach them. Used by IP to decide where to send a datagram or packet.

RSA

A public-key cryptographic algorithm named for its inventors (Rivest, Shamir, and Adleman) that does encryption and digital signatures.

RSVP

Resource Reservation Protocol.

SASL

Simple Authentication and Security Layer.

Schema

A name space and unit of ownership for a set of classes. Schemata may come in forms such as a text file, information in a repository, or diagrams in a CASE tool.

Scope

Part of a qualifier specification indicating with which meta-constructs the qualifier can be used. For example, the qualifier ABSTRACT has Scope(Class Association Indication), meaning that it can only be used with classes, associations and indications.

Scoping Object

Objects which represent a real-world managed element and in turn propagate keys to other objects.

Security Association

The security information that relates to a network connection or set of connections.

Security gateway

A system that provides security services and acts as the communications gateway between internal trusted hosts and subnets and external untrusted systems.

Sequenced Packet Exchange (SPX)

A connection-oriented protocol found in Novell NetWare networks. This transport layer protocol is similar to TCP and together with IPX, provides connection services similar to TCP/IP.

Shared Ethernet

An Ethernet configuration in which a number of segments are bound together in a single collision domain; hubs produce this type of configuration where only one node can transmit at a time.

Signature

The return type and parameters supported by a method.

Simple Network Management Protocol (SNMP)

Allows a TCP/IP host running an SNMP application to query other nodes for network-related statistics and error conditions; the other hosts, which provide SNMP agents, respond to these queries and allow a single host to gather network statistics from many other network nodes.

Single-Mode fiber

A type of fiber optic cable used for longer distances and higher speeds such as long-distance telephone lines. See also *multimode fiber*.

Single-line Digital Subscriber Line (SDSL)

SDSL is HDSL over a single twisted pair.

SLA

Service Level Agreement.

SNAP

Subnetwork Access Protocol.

SNMP

Simple Network Management Protocol.

Socket

An address that specifically includes a port identifier, that is, the concatenation of an Internet address with a TCP port.

SONET (Synchronous Optical Network)

A set of standard fiberoptic-based serial standards planned for use with ATM in North America; developed by Bellcore; different types of SONET run at different speeds, use different types of fiber, and operate over different distances. There are both single-mode and multimode fiber versions.

Spanning tree

An algorithm used to create a logical topology that connects all network segments, and ensures that only one path exists between any two nodes; a spanning tree is loop free and is a subset of a network. Multicast routers construct a spanning tree from the multicast source located at the root of the tree to all the members of the multicast group.

Sparse-mode multicast routing protocols

A category of routing protocol, sparse-mode routing protocols assume that the multicast group members are sparsely distributed throughout the network. The multicast group members could be distributed across many regions of the Internet. There can be just as many multicast group members in sparse-mode routing as there can be in dense-mode routing. Sparse-mode routing protocols include the Core Based Trees (CBT) and Protocol-Independent Multicast - Sparse Mode (PIM-SM) protocols. See also *dense-mode multicast routing protocols.*

SSL

Secure Sockets Layer.

Stream-oriented protocol

A type of protocol where data are organized as a stream of bytes, it uses a technique for transferring data so that data can be processed as a steady and continuous stream. With streaming, a client can start displaying the data before the entire file has been transmitted. If a client receives the data more quickly than required, he saves the excess data in a buffer. If the data do not come quickly enough, the presentation of the data is not smooth.

Subclass

See *Inheritance*.

Subnet

A portion of a network that shares a common address component; on TCP/IP networks, subnets are defined as all devices whose IP addresses have the same prefix. For example, all devices with IP addresses that start with 100.100.100. would be part of the same subnet. Dividing a network into subnets is useful for both security and performance reasons.

Superclass

See *Inheritance*.

Switch

A device that connects multiple network segments at the data-link layer (Layer 2) of the OSI model; switches operate more simply and at higher speeds than do routers.

Switched Multimegabit Data Service (SMDS)

High-speed, connectionless, packet-switched, WAN networking technology.

TCP/IP

Transmission Control Protocol/Internet Protocol.

TFTP

Trivial File Transfer Protocol.

Top Level Object

A class or object that has no scoping object.

ToS

Type of Service.

Transmission Control Protocol (TCP)

The protocol at the Internet's transport layer that governs the transmission of datagrams or packets by providing reliable, full-duplex, stream service to application protocols, especially IP. Provides reliable connection-oriented service by requiring that the sender and receiver exchange control information, or establish a connection before transmission can occur. Contrast to *User Datagram Protocol*.

Transport Service Access Point (TSAP)

The address that uniquely defines a particular instantiation of a service; formed by logically concatenating the node's NSAP with a transport identifier and sometimes a packet/protocol type.

Trigger

The occurrence of some action such as the creation, modification or deletion of an object, access to an object, or modification or access to a property. Triggers may also be fired as a result of the passage of a specified period of time. A trigger typically results in an *Indication*.

Tunneling

The practice of encapsulating a message from one protocol in another protocol and using the second protocol to traverse a number of network hops. At the destination, the encapsulation is stripped off and the original message is reintroduced to the network.

Twisted-pair

Telephone system cabling that consists of copper wires loosely twisted around each other to help cancel out any induced noise in balanced circuits.

UDP

User Datagram Protocol.

Unicast

The method of sending a packet or datagram to a single address; this type of point-to-point transmission requires the source to send an individual copy of a message to each requester. See also *anycast*, *multicast*, *broadcast*, and *IP multicasting*.

Universal Coordinated Time (UCT)

The number of seconds since 00:00 01/01/1970 Greenwich Mean Time.

URL

Uniform Resource Locator.

UTP

Unshielded twisted pair; one or more cable pairs surrounded by insulation; UTP is commonly used as telephone wire.

Variable MTU

A link that does not have a well-defined MTU, such as an IEEE 802.5 token-ring link. Many links, for example Ethernet links, have a standard MTU defined by the link-layer protocol or by the specific document describing how to run IP over the link layer.

Very high bit rate Digital Subscriber Line (VDSL)

A technology in which modems enable access and communications over twisted-pair lines at a data rate from 1.54 Mbps to 52 Mbps; VDSL has a maximum operating range from 1,000 feet to 4,500 feet on 24-gauge wire.

VLAN

Virtual LAN.

VPN

Virtual Private Network.

VRRP

Virtual Router Redundancy Protocol.

WFQ

Weighted Fair Queuing.

Wide Area Network (WAN)

A geographically dispersed network.

Window

One of the fundamental elements of the transport's state that can be controlled to affect the quality of service provided to the client; it represents the number of user-data carrying packets that may be multicast into the Web during a heartbeat by a single member.

XDSL

The "x" represents the various forms of digital subscriber line (DSL) technologies: ADSL, R-ADSL, HDSL, SDSL, or VDSL.

APPENDIX **B**

Bibliography

Aboba, B. "Lightweight Directory Access Protocol (v3): Dynamic Attributes for the Remote Access Dialin User Service (RADIUS)" Internet Draft (work in progress), draft-aboba-dynradius-01.txt, Microsoft, November 1997.

Aboba, B. "Lightweight Directory Access Protocol (v3): Extension for PPP Authentication" Internet Draft (work in progress), draft-aboba-ppp-01.txt, Microsoft, November 1997.

Aboba, B. "Lightweight Directory Access Protocol (v3): Schema for the Remote Access Dialin User Service (RADIUS) " Internet Draft (work in progress), draft-aboba-radius-01.txt, Microsoft, November 1997.

Blunk, L. J., and Vollbrecht, J. R. "PPP Extensible Authentication Protocol (EAP)." Work in progress, draft-ietf-pppext-eap-auth-02.txt, Merit Network, Inc., June 1996.

Booch, Grady and Rumbaugh, James "Unified Method for Object-Oriented Development Document Set", Rational Software Corporation, 1996. http://www.rational.com/uml

Calhoun, P., Rubens, A. C., and Aboba, B. "Extensible Authentication Protocol Support in RADIUS." Internet Draft (work in progress), draft-ietf-radius-eap-02.txt, 3Com, Merit Network, Microsoft, April 1997.

Calhoun, P.R., Beadles, M.A., and Ratcliffe, A. "RADIUS Accounting Interim Accounting Record Extension." Work in progress, draft-ietf- radius-acct-interim-00.txt, 3Com, CompuServe, UUNET, July 1997.

Carrel, D. and Grant, L. "The TACACS+ Protocol Version 1.77." Work in progress, draft-grant-tacacs-01.txt, Cisco Systems, October 1996.

"Code for the Representation of Names of Languages", ISO/IEC 639:1988 (E/F)

"Code for the Representation of Names of Territory", ISO/IEC 3166:1988 (E/F)

Coplein, James O., Schmidt, Douglas C (eds). Pattern Languages of Program Design, Reading MA: Addison-Wesley; 1995.

Gardarin, Georges and Valduriez, Patrick Relational Databases and Knowledge Bases, Reading, MA: Addison Wesley; 1989.

Hodges J., Morgan R.L., and Wahl M., "Lightweight Directory Access Protocol (v3): Extension for Transport Layer Security." Internet Draft (work in progress), draft-ietf-asid-ldapv3-tls-01.txt, Stanford, CA, Critical Angle, June 1997.

Howes, T., and Howard, L. "A Simple Caching Scheme for LDAP and X.500 Directories." Internet Draft (work in progress), draft-ietf-asidldap-cache-01.txt, Netscape, October 1997.

"IEEE Standard for Binary Floating-Point Arithmetic", ANSI/IEEE Standard 754-1985, Institute of Electrical and Electronics Engineers, Aug. 1985.

"Information Processing Systems - Open Systems Interconnection - The Directory: Overview of Concepts, Models and Service." ISO/IEC JTC 1/SC21, International Standard 9594-1, 1988.

"Information Processing Systems - Open Systems Interconnection - The Directory: Selected Object Classes." Recommendation X.521 ISO/IEC JTC 1/SC21, International Standard 9594-7, 1993.

Lloyd, B. and Simpson, W. "PPP Authentication Protocols", RFC 1334, L&A, DayDreamer, October 1992.

Miller, T. "Lightweight Directory Access Protocol (v3): Schema for Domain Name System", Internet Draft < id-miller-dns-ldap-schema.txt >, (work in progress)

Rigney, C. "RADIUS Accounting." RFC 2139, Livingston, April 1997.

Rigney, C., Rubens, A., Simpson, W., and Willens, S. "Remote Authentication Dial In User Service (RADIUS)." RFC 2138, Livingston, Merit, Daydreamer, April 1997.

Rigney, C. and Willats, W. "RADIUS Extensions." Work in progress, draft-ietf-radius-ext-01.txt, Livingston, June 1997.

Rivest, R., and Dusse, S."The MD5 Message-Digest Algorithm", RFC 1321, MIT Laboratory for Computer Science, RSA Data Security Inc., April 1992.

Simpson, W. "PPP Challenge Handshake Authentication Protocol (CHAP)", RFC 1994, August 1996.

Simpson, W., Ed. "The Point-to-Point Protocol (PPP)", STD 51, RFC 1661, July 1994.

UCS Transformation Format 8 (UTF-8), ISO/IEC 10646-1:1993 Amendment 2 (1996)

"The Unicode Standard, Version 2.0, by The Unicode Consortium" Addison-Wesley; Reading, MA: 1996.

Wahl,M., Coulbeck, A., Howes, T., and Kille, S. "Lightweight Directory Access Protocol (v3): Attribute Syntax Definitions. " Internet Draft (work in progress), draft-ietf-asid-ldapv3-attributes-08.txt, Critical Angle, Isode, Netscape, October 1997.

Wahl, M., Hoews, T., and Kille, S. "Lightweight Directory Access Protocol (v3)." Internet Draft (work in progress), draft-ietf-asid-protocol-08.txt, Critical Angle, Netscape, Isode, October 1997.

Yaacovi, Y., Wahl, M., and Genovese, T. "Lightweight Directory Access Protocol (v3): Extensions for Dynamic Directory Services. " Internet Draft (work in progress), draft-ietf-asid-ldapv3-dynamic-06.txt, Microsoft, Critical Angle, September 1997.

Yaacovi, Y., Wahl, M., and Genovese, T. "Lightweight Directory Access Protocol: Dynamic Attributes." Internet Draft (work in progress), draft-ietf-asid-dynatt-00.txt, Microsoft, Critical Angle, July 1997.

Yeong, W., Howes, T., and Kille, S. "Lightweight Directory Access Protocol." RFC 1777, March 1995.

RFC 2131 – Droms, R. "Dynamic Host Configuration Protocol", RFC 2131, March 1997.

RFC 2132 – Alexander, S. and Droms, R. "DHCP Options and BOOTP Vendor Extensions", RFC 2132, Mar. 1997.

RFC 2234 – Augmented BNF for Syntax Specifications: ABNF, Nov. 1997.

RFC 2241 – Provan, D. "DHCP Options for Novell Directory Services", RFC 2241, November 1997.

RFC 2242 – Droms, R. and Fong, K. "NetWare/IP Domain Name and Information", RFC 2242, November 1997.

RFC 2252 – Wahl, M., Coulbeck, A., Howles, T., and Kille, S. "Lightweight Directory Access Protocol (v3): Attribute Syntax Definitions, RFC 2252, December 1997.

Index